CONTENTS

Workbook

HOW 7

Seventh Edition

A Handbook for Office Workers

James L. Clark
Chairman, Business Department
Pasadena City College

Lyn R. Clark
Professor, Office Administration Department
Los Angeles Pierce College

SOUTH-WESTERN College Publishing

An International Thomson Publishing Company

Sponsoring Editor: Gary Bauer
Developmental Editor: Tom Bormann
Production Editor: Tracy Megison
Production House: Julia Chitwood
Designer: Joseph M. Devine
Marketing Manager: Dreis Van Landuyt
Manufacturing Coordinator: Karen Truman

KF60GD

Copyright © 1995
by South-Western College Publishing
Cincinnati, Ohio

ISBN: 0-538-85043-4
1 2 3 4 5 6 7 8 9 PN 2 1 0 9 8 7 6 5 4
Printed in the United States of America

International Thomson Publishing
South-Western College Publishing is an ITP Company. The ITP trademark is used
under license.

PREFACE

The worksheets in this book, *Workbook for HOW 7,* have been developed to correlate specifically with the principles in *HOW 7: A Handbook for Office Workers,* Seventh Edition. Each section in this workbook corresponds with a specific chapter in *HOW 7.* In fact, the section references containing the information needed to complete each worksheet are shown in parentheses in the introductory heading.

Workbook for HOW 7 is divided into eight sections. Instructions for completing the worksheets in each section precede the exercise materials. Answers or solutions to the initial learning activity are given in the concluding pages of the workbook. Other keys and solutions are contained in the *Instructor's Manual and Key for HOW 7.* The worksheets are perforated so that they may be removed from the book and turned in to the instructor.

Students may use this workbook independently, or they may use it as an organized class activity. If the worksheets are to be completed independently, the students should first complete the Familiarization Exercise presented on pages 3 to 11. Then, they should use the information presented in *HOW 7* to complete the worksheets.

If *Workbook for HOW 7* is to be used as a regular classroom learning activity, the transparency masters contained in the instructor's manual may be used to present the major principles before the corresponding worksheets are completed.

Additional ideas for using this workbook may be found in the *Instructor's Manual and Key for HOW 7.* For example, the exercises appearing in Sections 1, 3, and 4 of the workbook may be used in conjunction with the sets of business letter and memorandum problems contained in Part 4 of the instructor's manual. Regardless of the instructional methods employed, however, the practice materials contained in *Workbook for HOW 7* will reinforce the knowledge and skills needed to prepare business documents.

Part 1

Familiarization Exercise for HOW

Instructions: Use HOW to locate the correct answers to the following items. Place the letter or letters corresponding with the correct answer in the answer column provided. Indicate in the second column the number of the section (or page number when no section number is given) where you found your answer. When you have completed this exercise, check your answers with those on page 209.

Answer   Section

1. In looking up solutions for problems in HOW, which of the following would you consult first?
   a. Index
   b. Solution Finder
   c. Back cover
   d. Table of Contents   _____ _____

2. If you are unable to locate needed information because you do not know the name of the chapter in which it might be contained, which section of HOW would you consult?
   a. Table of Contents
   b. Solution Finder
   c. Preface
   d. Index   _____ _____

3. The tabbed cardstock chapter dividers are used for
   a. Making HOW more attractive.
   b. Locating the Solution Finder for each chapter.
   c. Referring to the Table of Contents.
   d. Locating specific chapters from the Index.   _____ _____

4. Which of the following is the most efficient plan recommended by the authors to locate information in HOW?
   a. Consult Table of Contents, turn to page listing for chapter needed, and use Solution Finder to locate specific section that contains answer.
   b. Turn to back cover, locate chapter needed, use tabbed cardstock chapter divider to reach Solution Finder, and use Solution Finder to locate specific section that contains answer.
   c. Turn to Index, locate major heading in Index, locate topic under major heading, and use tabbed cardstock divider to locate chapter and specific section.   _____ _____

5. Which of the plans described in Question 4 should be used if the information cannot be located through the chapter titles?   _____ _____

6. If you wanted to know how to address a letter to the mayor of your city, which chapter would you consult?
   a. Capitalization
   b. Business Letters and Memorandums
   c. Address Format and Forms of Address
   d. Literary and Artistic Titles   _____ _____

7. If you had a parcel to mail for your company, which chapter would you consult to assist you?
   a. Office Application Skills
   b. Message Transmission Media
   c. Business Letters and Memorandums
   d. Address Format and Forms of Address

8. If you wanted to locate information on setting up a letter using a word processing program, which chapter should you consult?
   a. Office Application Skills
   b. Business Letters and Memorandums
   c. Document Formats and Terminology in the Automated Office
   d. Message Transmission Media

9. If you had looked in the chapter "Business Letters and Memorandums" and could not locate information for formatting a business letter on a word processing program, where next would you look to find this material?
   a. Index
   b. Table of Contents
   c. Back cover
   d. Another Solution Finder

10. If you wanted to know whether a word in a letter should be spelled *affect* or *effect,* which chapter of HOW would you consult?
    a. Grammar and Usage
    b. Office Application Skills
    c. Hyphenating and Dividing Words
    d. Words Often Misused and Confused

11. Which one of the following sentences is punctuated correctly?
    a. Will you please send us your check by the end of the month?
    b. Will you please send us your check by the end of the month.

12. Business organizations and divisions are usually divided into departments. How would you handle the capitalization of department names? Indicate which of the following sentences are correct. Select all correct answers.
    a. Our personnel department hired three new accountants today.
    b. Our Department is planning to enlarge its facilities.
    c. We will send the forms to the Research Department next week.
    d. When can we expect to receive the reports from the Accounting Department?

13. Related numbers are handled similarly in the same format. According to HOW, which of the sentences below have been expressed correctly? Select all correct answers.
    a. Our 4 salespersons sold 32 houses this week.
    b. We will be able to fill your order for 26 chairs, 9 dining tables, and 4 sofas.

    c. Of the 12 entrees listed, only four were priced under $10.

    d. Last year our subscribers increased from 2 million to 2,800,000.

    _____ _____

14. Some compound numbers are always hyphenated; others are not. Locate the correct rule in HOW. Then indicate which of the following numbers are expressed correctly. Select all correct answers.
    a. twenty seven
    b. one hundred nineteen
    c. eighty-three
    d. two hundred fifty-seven
    e. one-hundred forty-three

    _____ _____

15. Pronouns are used in the subjective case under certain circumstances. Select all the correct circumstances from the ones described below.
    a. As the complement of a "being" verb
    b. Following a preposition
    c. As the subject of a sentence
    d. After *to be* when this infinitive does not have a subject
    e. As the subject of any infinitive other than *to be*

    _____ _____

16. In comparing adjectives, which of the following sentences are written correctly? Select all correct answers.
    a. John writes letters more better than I.
    b. This men's suit line is the most handsome one I have seen this season.
    c. Our reception area is more cheery since it has been redecorated.
    d. The hard disk on your computer is more nearly full than the one on mine.

    _____ _____

17. Which of the following geographical locations are expressed correctly? Select all correct answers.
    a. Our next flight to New York City will leave at 10:05 a.m.
    b. We took float trips down the Colorado and Snake rivers.
    c. Last year the State of Colorado initiated new election procedures.
    d. Most of our new business has come from the South.

    _____ _____

18. Select the correct format or formats for expressing the name of the following book. Select all correct answers.
    a. *How: A Handbook For Office Workers*
    b. HOW: A Handbook for Office Workers
    c. How: a Handbook for Office Workers
    d. <u>HOW: A Handbook for Office Workers</u>
    e. *HOW: A Handbook for Office Workers*
    f. HOW: A HANDBOOK FOR OFFICE WORKERS

    _____ _____

19. Which one of the following sentences has been punctuated correctly?
    a. "All overtime work has been canceled", said Mr. Stevens.
    b. "All overtime work has been canceled" said Mr. Stevens.
    c. "All overtime work has been canceled," said Mr. Stevens.
    d. "All overtime work has been canceled;" said Mr. Stevens.

    _____ _____

20. Which one of the following sentences has been punctuated correctly?
    a. You may wish in addition, to order from our new catalog.
    b. You may wish, in addition, to order from our new catalog.
    c. You may wish in addition to order from our new catalog.
    d. You may wish in addition; to order from our new catalog.

21. If you were asked to address a letter to R. Lewis, how would you begin the salutation? According to HOW, which of the following salutations would be correct? Select all correct answers.
    a. Dear Mr. Lewis
    b. Dear R. Lewis
    c. Dear Mrs. Lewis
    d. Dear Ms. Lewis

22. According to the rules for forming noun plurals, which of the following words are spelled correctly? Select all correct choices.
    a. attornies   d. monies
    b. notaries   e. companys
    c. valleys   f. secretarys

23. Which of the following uses of *among* and *between* are correct? Select all correct choices.
    a. Please distribute these supplies among the two departments.
    b. This information should remain between the three of us.
    c. Place the lamp between the two tables.
    d. The invoice was found among the legal documents.

24. Locate in HOW the correct rule for capitalizing words following a colon. Which one of the following sentences is correct?
    a. With our next order please ship the following: Three copies of the invoice, a copy of your new catalog, and instructions for returning merchandise.
    b. With our next order please ship the following: three copies of the invoice, a copy of your new catalog, and instructions for returning merchandise.
    c. With our next order please ship the following: Three copies of the invoice. A copy of your new catalog. Instructions for returning merchandise.

25. There are specific rules regarding subject-verb agreement for sentences beginning with *There* and subjects indicating portions. Locate this section in HOW. From it determine which of the sentences are using the principles correctly. Select all correct choices.
    a. There is three people in the lobby waiting to see Dr. Lyons.
    b. About one half of the packages has been shipped.
    c. There is only one blank check left in the book.
    d. Some of the contracts have been destroyed in the fire.

FAMILIARIZATION EXERCISE FOR HOW

26. Which one of the following sentences is punctuated correctly?
    a. Our new line of fleet cars has power steering, cruise control, and automatic windows.
    b. Our new line of fleet cars has power steering; cruise control; and automatic windows.
    c. Our new line of fleet cars has power steering, cruise control and automatic windows.
    d. Our new line of fleet cars has power steering; cruise control and automatic windows.

    _____ _____

27. Which date is expressed correctly?
    a. Please send us your check by March 22nd.
    b. We must have your check by the 22 of March.
    c. The audit was conducted on March 22nd, 1995.
    d. May we have your reply by March 22.

    _____ _____

28. In the modified block letter style, the date may be placed in all the positions listed below except one. Use HOW to determine which one of the positions listed below is incorrect.
    a. Aligned with (pivoted from) the right margin
    b. Centered
    c. Begun at the center of the page
    d. Begun at the left margin

    _____ _____

29. Which of the following statements are true about dividing words at the end of a line? Select all correct choices.
    a. The last words appearing in two consecutive lines in the middle of a paragraph may not be divided.
    b. The last word of a paragraph may never be divided.
    c. The last word appearing on a page may never be divided.
    d. The last word in the first line of a paragraph may never be divided.

    _____ _____

30. Sometimes professional titles are capitalized; other times they are not. Which of the following sentences are written correctly? Select all correct choices.
    a. May I please have an appointment to see the President of your company?
    b. Please ask Professor Ripley to call me.
    c. Sally Abramowitz, the President of Allied Enterprises, attended the conference.
    d. Yes, we did receive a response from the vice president of the United States.

    _____ _____

31. Which of the following uses of *principal* and *principle* are correct? Select all correct choices.
    a. The principle of our school resigned yesterday.
    b. You must reinvest the principal within 90 days.
    c. Please take time to review these accounting principals.
    d. My principle concern is that we retain the same high quality in our products.

    _____ _____

32. Sometimes nouns appearing with numbers or letters are capitalized; other times they are not. Which of the following sentences are written correctly? Select all correct choices.
    a. Please return policy 381294 to us in the enclosed envelope.
    b. Ask Ms. Mann to delete line 5 from the first paragraph.
    c. Our committee plans to meet in Room 52 at 1:30 p.m.
    d. The graph was located on Page 4.

    _____ _____

33. Which one of the following dates is punctuated correctly?
    a. By August 15, we must complete our inventory.
    b. By August 15, 1996 we must complete our inventory.
    c. By Tuesday August 15, 1996, we must complete our inventory.
    d. By Tuesday, August 15, 1996, we must complete our inventory.

    _____ _____

34. Sometimes compound adjectives are hyphenated; other times they are not. From the information contained in HOW, indicate which sentences are correct. Select all correct choices.
    a. Your thoroughly-documented report has been read by the research staff.
    b. Because your records are up-to-date, we have been able to contact members who have not paid this year's annual dues.
    c. Use 4- by 6-inch cards for this invitation.
    d. Only three high-school students applied for the scholarship.

    _____ _____

35. Which of the following statements are true about the placement of an attention line in a letter? Select all correct choices.
    a. The attention line may be typed after the salutation.
    b. The attention line may be included in the inside address.
    c. The attention line must always be underlined.
    d. The attention line may or may not be followed by a colon.

    _____ _____

36. Which of the following words *may not* or *should not* be divided at the end of a line? Select all correct choices.
    a. counter   e. February 25
    b. preface   f. solo
    c. constant   g. Massachusetts
    d. thought   h. kindness

    _____ _____

37. What are the dimensions of a No. 10 envelope?
    a. 6 1/2 inches x 3 5/8 inches
    b. 9 1/2 inches x 4 1/8 inches
    c. 7 1/2 inches x 3 7/8 inches
    d. 5 15/16 inches x 4 5/8 inches

    _____ _____

38. Which group of numbers in the following choices is always expressed in figures?
    a. Amounts of money, percentages, weights and measures
    b. Dates, periods of time, amounts of money
    c. Clock time, telephone numbers, percentages
    d. Fractions, numbers at the beginning of a sentence, zip codes

    _____ _____

39. If you were to write the governor of your state, which form of
address would you use for the salutation?
    a. Dear Mr. Harris:
    b. Dear Governor:
    c. Esteemed Honorable Sir:
    d. Dear Governor Harris:
    e. Dear Excellency:

40. Which of the following statements are true about placing
mailing notations in a business letter? Select all correct
choices.
    a. Mailing notations always appear in all capital letters.
    b. Mailing notations may appear in a combination of
       uppercase and lowercase letters OR in all capital letters.
    c. Mailing notations may appear a double space below the
       date.
    d. Mailing notations may appear a double space above the
       inside address.
    e. Mailing notations may appear directly below the copy
       notation.

41. Most verbs form their parts in a regular way (*ask, asked,
asked*). Others, though, do not follow the regular pattern. On
the basis of the information contained in HOW, indicate which
of the combinations given below are correct. Select all correct
choices.
    a. go   went   gone
    b. catch   catched   catched
    c. pay   payed   payed
    d. do   done   done
    e. throw   threw   thrown

42. Which of the following sentences are correct in their handling
of academic subjects, courses, or degrees? Select all correct
choices.
    a. Will you enroll in History 12 this semester?
    b. I plan to take a course in Mathematical Analysis.
    c. When will you earn your Associate in Arts degree?
    d. What grade did you earn in your conversational Spanish
       class?

43. Second-page headings for business letters and memorandums
include the following information:
    a. Complete address of addressee
    b. Page number only, centered
    c. Name of addressee, name of sender, page number
    d. Name of addressee, page number, date

44. Which of the following amounts of money are expressed correctly? Select all correct choices.
    a. We received invoices for $101.87, $395.00, and $62.50 today.
    b. The postage for your two packages was 87 cents and $1.73.
    c. Has the retail price of your pens increased from 89 cents to 99 cents?
    d. The construction costs for this building were estimated to be $3,000,000.

    _____ _____

45. Which of the following uses of *affect* and *effect* are correct? Select all correct choices.
    a. Will the price increase affect our sales volume?
    b. The lower property taxes will certainly effect our profits for this year.
    c. What effect did the medicine have on Mr. Reed's heart?
    d. He plans to effect several changes in our constitution and bylaws.

    _____ _____

46. Which of the following movie titles are expressed correctly? Select all correct choices.
    a. Next week "Gone With the Wind" will be shown on television.
    b. Next week Gone With the Wind will be shown on television.
    c. Next week GONE WITH THE WIND will be shown on television.
    d. Next week *Gone With the Wind* will be shown on television.

    _____ _____

47. According to the general rules for expressing numbers, which of the following statements are true? Select all correct choices.
    a. Numbers *ten* and below are usually written in word form; numbers above *ten* are usually written in figure form.
    b. Approximations above *ten* are always written in figures.
    c. Numbers above *ten* may not be used to begin a sentence.
    d. Round numbers in the millions or billions are usually expressed in a combination of figures and words.

    _____ _____

48. Which one of the following compound sentences is punctuated correctly?
    a. All our salespersons are attending a sales meeting in Chicago, therefore, no one will be available to call on your company until next week.
    b. All our salespersons are attending a sales meeting in Chicago, therefore no one will be available to call on your company until next week.
    c. All our salespersons are attending a sales meeting in Chicago; therefore no one will be available to call on your company until next week.
    d. All our salespersons are attending a sales meeting in Chicago; therefore, no one will be available to call on your company until next week.

    _____ _____

49. Which of the following statements are **not** true about forming possessives? Select all correct choices.
   a. Nouns not ending with a pronounced "s" form the possessive by adding *'s.*
   b. All nouns may show possession.
   c. When two or more persons own a single item, show possession only on the last person.
   d. Ownership on compound nouns is shown on the main word, i.e., *sister's-in-law.*

   _____ _____

50. Which of the following uses of *lose* and *loose* are correct? Select all correct choices.
   a. Did you loose any money in the stock market this year?
   b. The paper guide on this printer is loose.
   c. When did you lose your watch?
   d. This lose screw must be tightened.

   _____ _____

Check your answers with those given on page 209.

Part 2

...ation

The ....contain 19 sets of exercises for each of the major uses of the comma, the s.......... ...he colon. These sets include *Practice Sentences*, a *Practice Paragraph*, and a ....ent *Letter*.

Each princ...e is labeled by name at the beginning of the exercise series. The section in HOW that explains the use of the principle is shown in parentheses.

For *Practice Sentences* use revision marks to insert the commas where they are needed. Only commas illustrating the principle under consideration are used. After you have placed commas where they are needed, check your answers on pages 211–218.

Practice Paragraphs use mainly those cor........ ...presented in the current section. Insert the necessary commas and *label them usin.............. ...viations listed below*. Then check your answers on pages 211–218.

Punctuation Labels

Comma:

			...	omit
Series	ser			cl
Parenthetical	par	Sho... ...ation		sq
Direct Address	da	**Semicolon:**		
Apposition	app	No Conjunction		nc
Date	date	Coordinating Conjunction		cc
Address	add	Transitional Expression		trans
Coordinating Conjunction	cc	Series		ser
Independent Adjective	ia	Enumerations		enum
Introductory Clause	intro	**Colon:**		
Introductory Phrase	intro	Enumerated or Listed Items		list
Nonrestrictive	nr	Explanatory Sentence		exp
Contrasting Expression	cont ex			

An illustration of an edited *Practice Paragraph* appears below:

     We, of course, are concerned about the production problems Deco Designs has

encountered during the past year. We cannot, however, allow its unpaid balance of $324 to

continue much longer. You can perhaps understand the difficult position suppliers find themselves in today. We too *par* must meet our financial obligations. Therefore *par* we must turn

over this account for collection unless we receive payment by May 1.

Reinforcement Letters are cumulative; that is, once a punctuation principle has been covered in a previous exercise, it may appear in any of the following *Reinforcement Letters.* For the *Reinforcement Letters* insert the necessary punctuation marks and label each mark using the abbreviations given previously. Check your answers with your instructor. An example of an edited *Reinforcement Letter* follows:

Dear Ms. Davis:

We appreciate receiving your April 8 letter. Because we want you to be pleased with

your selection for many years to come, *intro* your china is available on an open-stock basis. If you

need to replace a broken piece, *intro* you may do so at any time. Also, *par* you may purchase additional

pieces at your convenience.

Enclosed is a brochure describing your china pattern. This brochure features the

available moneysaving sets, *cc* and it also shows all pieces that may be purchased individually.

If you are interested in purchasing additional sets or individual pieces, *intro* use the enclosed order

form. You may include a check with your order, *ser* charge it on a bankcard, *ser* or have it sent c.o.d.

We hope this information has been helpful to you. However, *intro* if you have any other

questions, *intro* please let us know.

Sincerely yours,

Comma Placement, Series (1-1)

Practice Sentences 1

1. The latest weather reports show rain sleet and ice in New York City.

2. The administrative assistant in our office uses a word processor prepares spreadsheets and answers numerous telephone inquiries.

3. This particular travel group is scheduled to tour Arizona Nevada Utah and Montana.

4. We changed all the locks barred the outside windows and installed a burglar alarm system last week.

5. Trees shrubs and ground cover are needed to complete this project.

6. Call Henry Smith offer him the job and ask him to begin work July 1.

7. Many doctors dentists and lawyers are among our clientele.

8. The contractor obtained a permit purchased the building materials and hired several additional workers to complete the job within the specified three-week period.

9. Proofread the report make three copies and mail the original to Ms. Williams.

10. Sheila was late because she stopped at the stationery store post office and grocery store before reporting to work.

Check your answers with those given on page 211 before completing the following exercise.

Practice Paragraph 1

We must correspond with Mr. Jones regarding our inventory sales and profit picture. Ask him to let us know how our high inventory low sales volume and declining profits during the last quarter will affect our status for the entire year. Write the letter sign it and mail it.

Check your answers with those given on page 211 before completing the following exercise.

Reinforcement Letter 1

To: John Cole

Our assistant collected the facts Mr. Phillips researched the case and Ms. Watson prepared the brief. This team of experts was instrumental in our receiving a favorable court decision. They are to be congratulated on their ability patience and success.

Please continue to rely on Mr. Day for collecting the information Mr. Phillips for conducting the research and Ms. Watson for preparing the briefs. We will be able to develop a steady group of business industrial and professional clients by using the special talents of these three people.

*The answers to this exercise appear in the **Instructor's Manual and Key for HOW 7: A Handbook for Office Workers, Seventh Edition.***

Comma Placement, Parenthetical (1-2)

Practice Sentences 2

1. In fact Mr. Ryan has called our office several times.

2. We feel nevertheless that you should honor your original commitment.

3. The committee has rejected his proposal fortunately.

4. Yes we are planning to revise the previous edition.

5. The chapter was not in other words well presented and thoroughly documented.

6. Between you and me I would be surprised if Canton Industries bids on this project.

7. We are therefore closing your account until the overdue balance has been paid.

8. We will have your order shipped to you in time for your fall sale without a doubt.

9. Perhaps you would like to purchase this set of encyclopedias on a free 10-day trial basis.

10. You can indeed receive a full refund within 30 days if you are not fully satisfied with any of our products.

Check your answers with those given on page 211 before completing the following exercise.

Practice Paragraph 2

We as a rule do not employ inexperienced accountants. However Mr. Williams has so many excellent recommendations that we could not afford to turn down his application. Perhaps you will wish to meet him personally before assigning him to a supervisor. I can of course have him stop by your office tomorrow.

Check your answers with those given on page 211 before completing the following exercise.

Reinforcement Letter 2

To: David Post

Next month we will open new stores in Los Angeles San Francisco and Phoenix. Publicity releases consequently have already been sent to the major newspapers in these cities. In addition we will advertise a number of grand opening specials that should attract a large number of customers.

Plans for opening our new stores are contained in the attached report. You may however wish to contact the store managers for further information on their sales promotions their present inventory of merchandise and their progress in hiring personnel. Some additional information will perhaps be of help to you in your new assignment.

Your assistance needless to say will be important in assessing marketing trends in Los Angeles San Francisco and Phoenix. May we rely on you then for information regarding consumer preferences buying habits and purchasing power? The results of your research will indeed assist the staff in ensuring the success of these three new stores.

The answers to this exercise appear in the **Instructor's Manual and Key for HOW 7: A Handbook for Office Workers, Seventh Edition.**

Comma Placement, Direct Address (1-3)

Practice Sentences 3

1. Brett please reword the final paragraph of this letter to refer to the enclosures.

2. You may continue class with the assigned lessons shown in your syllabus.

3. Your staff is certainly efficient Mrs. Davis.

4. We can ladies and gentlemen promise you increased dividends for the next fiscal period.

5. Have you Gary decided on the dates for your vacation this year?

6. Yes fellow citizens of Spokane Senator Winfield's voting record is open for public scrutiny.

7. We plan to ask Ms. Stevens to complete the billing for this month.

8. Only you can help us solve this problem Dr. Bush.

9. Will David Kloss be leaving for Michigan next week?

10. Only you friends and neighbors can prevent further crime increases in this city.

Check your answers with those given on pages 211–212 before completing the following exercise.

Practice Paragraph 3

Would you Ms. White please review the financial report. I would appreciate your doing so too Ms. Smith. Gentlemen please check with both Ms. White and Ms. Smith for their advice before making any further financial commitments.

Check your answers with those given on page 212 before completing the following exercise.

Reinforcement Letter 3

Dear Mrs. Smith:

We welcome you as a charge account customer of the Valley Department Store. Enclosed are your two charge account plates some information outlining our charge plan and a circular describing our special sale items for this month.

You may be interested Mrs. Smith in the special dress sale now in progress. In fact this sale is one of the best we have had this year. You can for example purchase many of our designer clothes at half price. We hope that you will be able to take advantage of these savings.

Sincerely yours,

*The answers to this exercise appear in the **Instructor's Manual and Key for HOW 7: A Handbook for Office Workers, Seventh Edition.***

Comma Placement, Appositives (1-4)

Practice Sentences 4

1. This new budget was proposed by our accountant Stan Hughes last week.

2. John's sister the author of a best-seller has agreed to speak at one of our association meetings.

3. Senator Johnson a member of the finance committee favors our position.

4. John J. Lopez Jr. has requested our committee to provide new funds for his program.

5. Was your latest article "Skiing in California" accepted for publication?

6. Is it possible that they themselves are not confident of the outcome?

7. Janet Hodges our new assistant will be working in the office next to yours.

8. This book was written by Alice Porter and David Simms two prominent authorities on the subject of consumer finance.

9. Please refer any requests for further information to my assistant Bill.

10. One of our new clients Crutchfield Industries has recently been admitted to the New York Stock Exchange.

Check your answers with those given on page 212 before completing the following exercise.

Practice Paragraph 4

We have just learned that our president Mr. Black will retire next June. He has been president of Data Products Inc. for the past ten years. My assistant received the news yesterday and believes that Stephen Gold Ph.D. will be asked to fill the position. We will keep our employees informed of further developments through our monthly newsletter *Data Jottings.*

Check your answers with those given on page 212 before completing the following exercise.

Reinforcement Letter 4

Dear Mr. Ray:

Our newest project in the business communication area *Writing Résumés That Get Jobs* will be released within the next three months. Consequently we are in the process of preparing an advertising campaign for these materials. One of the authors James Martin Jr. will be contacting you shortly about the special features of this program.

The authors editors and reviewers all expect this book to be one of our best-sellers next year. There has been a need for a book of this type for some time. Hopefully our potential customers will recognize the considerable amount of effort that has gone into producing the kind of book for which they have indicated a need.

Mr. Sharp our advertising manager has asked his son Peter to work up some preliminary drawings for the artwork to advertise this new book. Peter has had considerable experience in this area and has done some other freelance work for our organization.

We will be able to meet with Peter as soon as he has had an opportunity to work up the preliminary drawings. He himself is not exactly sure when he can have them available. However I will contact you regarding a specific date time and place when we are ready for the initial conference.

Sincerely yours,

The answers to this exercise appear in the **Instructor's Manual and Key for HOW 7: A Handbook for Office Workers, Seventh Edition.**

Comma Placement, Dates and Time Zones (1-5)

Practice Sentences 5

1. The merger took place on February 28 1995.

2. On April 18 we will expect to receive your check for $720 to cover your overdue account.

3. Did you say that the president's address will be broadcast at 9 p.m. EST?

4. The contractor expects the building to be completed by October 1997.

5. We have made arrangements for the conference to be held on Thursday June 12 1996.

6. By April 15 the bulk of our income tax work will have been completed.

7. Our records show that on November 4 1994 your association filed for tax-exempt status.

8. Your subscription to this vital magazine ends with the July 1997 issue.

9. USAir Flight 390 is scheduled to land in Los Angeles at 8:40 a.m. PST.

10. On Wednesday December 6 1997 the company will have been in business for a century.

Check your answers with those given on page 212 before completing the following exercise.

Practice Paragraph 5

We will meet on April 1 to plan the scheduled opening of two new branch offices on Tuesday May 3 and Thursday May 19. These offices are the first ones we have opened since August 22 1994. We will need to plan these openings carefully because we will be directly responsible for two additional openings in September 1997 and April 1998.

Check your answers with those given on page 212 before completing the following exercise.

Reinforcement Letter 5

Dear Charles:

We are pleased to announce that the next convention for hotel managers will be held from Tuesday September 30 1997 until Friday October 3 1997 at the West Hotel in Chicago.

The convention committee recognizes that the next convention was originally scheduled for September 1998. However the convention committee felt that the date should be moved forward since so many of our members had expressed an interest in meeting annually. We hope Charles that this change in convention plans will fit into your schedule.

We would very much like to have you speak at one of our morning meetings. Ed Bates our program chairman suggested that you might be interested in describing the new reservations plan you developed for the Holiday Hotels. Would you be able to address the membership on this topic on October 2?

Please let me know as soon as possible if you will be able to accept this invitation.

Sincerely,

*The answers to this exercise appear in the **Instructor's Manual and Key for HOW 7: A Handbook for Office Workers, Seventh Edition.***

Comma Placement, Addresses (1-6)

Practice Sentences 6

1. Please return this application to Los Angeles Pierce College 6201 Winnetka Avenue Woodland Hills California 91371.

2. Mrs. Harvey presently resides at 221 Spring Street Los Angeles California 90001.

3. We will tour London England and Paris France during our travels.

4. Our company owns a number of condominium complexes in Honolulu Hawaii.

5. The tour agent sold us tickets to Albuquerque New Mexico in error.

6. The closest branch office is located at 569 Tiffany Lane Knoxville Tennessee 37912.

7. Please complete this form and send it to Mrs. Alice Stocker Office Manager Smythe & Ryan Investment Counselors 632 Raven Boulevard Suite 104 Baltimore Maryland 21239.

8. This customer's new address is Box 1530 Rural Route 2 Bangor Maine 55810.

9. Dallas Texas has been selected as the site for our 1998 convention.

10. All these articles are imported from Madrid Spain.

Check your answers with those given on pages 212–213 before completing the following exercise.

Practice Paragraph 6

We sent the information to Mr. David Hope Manager Larry's Clothing Store 1853 Fountain Avenue Atlanta Georgia 30314. The information should have been sent to Mr. Hope's new address in Columbus Ohio. It is 9653 Third Avenue Columbus Ohio 43203.

Check your answers with those given on page 213 before completing the following exercise.

Reinforcement Letter 6

Gentlemen:

Please reserve for me two gift subscriptions under your special holiday plan. These subscriptions are for one year and should begin with your January 1997 issue.

One gift subscription should be sent to Mrs. Alice Daily 361 Victory Avenue Boston Massachusetts 02101. The other one should be sent to Mrs. Ann Green 4923 West 85 Street Pittsburgh Pennsylvania 15230.

I would appreciate your sending the bill for these subscriptions to my office. The address is Tower Building Suite 201 2098 Washington Street San Francisco California 94101.

Please acknowledge receipt of this order. In addition I would appreciate your sending gift cards to both Mrs. Daily and Mrs. Green telling them of their gift subscriptions that are to begin on January 1 1997.

Sincerely yours,

The answers to this exercise appear in the **Instructor's Manual and Key for HOW 7: A Handbook for Office Workers, Seventh Edition.**

Comma Placement, Coordinating Conjunctions (1-7)

Practice Sentences 7

1. Three major accounting reports are due in January and two of them must be prepared for presentation to the Board of Directors.

2. The meeting was scheduled to adjourn at 3 p.m. but we had not finished all the business by then.

3. You may transfer to our Chicago office or you may remain here in Cincinnati.

4. Most of the applicants cannot keyboard well nor can they use our word processing program.

5. Marie was offered a promotion last week but did not accept it.

6. A new edition of this textbook has been published and it will be available in the spring.

7. We hope that Mr. Moore will be able to attend the convention and that he will be our guest for the banquet on May 5.

8. Tom will finish the project himself or he will arrange for his assistant to complete it.

9. Bob will not have to travel to Akron nor will he have to move out of this district.

10. Janet has been promoted twice and is now eligible for a third advancement.

Check your answers with those given on page 213 before completing the following exercise.

Practice Paragraph 7

We have checked our records and find that you are correct. Our deposit was mailed to your branch office but no record of this deposit was entered into our check record. Our records have been corrected and we appreciate your help in solving this problem. We hope that we have not caused you any inconvenience and that we may rely upon your help in the future.

Check your answers with those given on page 213 before completing the following exercise.

Reinforcement Letter 7

Dear Mr. Harris:

We are pleased to announce that in the near future we will be opening several new branch offices. The first one is scheduled to open in Tacoma Washington on June 1 1996. Other offices are planned for Indianapolis Indiana and Tampa Florida.

You may mail all future orders to the Tacoma office and we will fill these orders from there. Just fill out one of the enclosed order blanks and your order will be processed immediately upon receipt. We plan to serve our customers more rapidly and efficiently in this way.

Mr. Parks the former manager of our Portland branch will be in charge of the Tacoma office. He will be able to assist you with future orders and follow through on their delivery. We cannot promise you a three-day delivery date for regular orders but I can assure you that most orders will reach you within a week. Of course we will continue to provide our express overnight service for an additional shipping fee.

We hope that you will take advantage of ordering from our Tacoma office and that this new development in our company will hasten deliveries to your store.

Sincerely yours,

*The answers to this exercise appear in the **Instructor's Manual and Key for HOW 7: A Handbook for Office Workers, Seventh Edition.***

Comma Placement, Independent Adjectives (1-8)

Practice Sentences 8

1. Mr. Sommers is known to be a pleasant patient supervisor.

2. Was your real estate agent able to locate an affordable five-bedroom home for the Lopezes?

3. The red brick building on the corner of Main and Third Streets is scheduled to be demolished next week.

4. The Hardys own an elegant secluded restaurant in the Berkshires.

5. This afternoon one of the customers broke an expensive crystal vase.

6. Ms. Rice's ambitious greedy attitude made the other agents uneasy.

7. Our new filing system has caused considerable confusion.

8. Your outgoing cheerful manner has brought you many friends.

9. One of our wealthy well-known alumni has donated $1 million to our new library wing.

10. We still need to purchase a walnut secretarial desk for the reception area.

Check your answers with those given on page 213 before completing the following exercise.

Practice Paragraph 8

Your informative well-written report was submitted to the board of education yesterday. You will certainly be permitted to purchase some inexpensive modern equipment on the basis of the facts presented. I am sure the board will agree that the present facilities do not reflect a realistic practical learning environment for business students.

Check your answers with those given on page 213 before completing the following exercise.

Reinforcement Letter 8

Dear Mr. Winters:

I am pleased to recommend John Davis for a position with your accounting firm. He has been in our employ for three years and we are sorry to see him leave our company.

Mr. Davis is an intelligent hardworking young man. His pleasant congenial manner has also contributed to our organization. Unfortunately our small company is unable to offer him the opportunities for advancement to which a person of his ability is entitled.

Mr. Davis has been in charge of accounts receivable for the last year. His duties included posting purchases to individual accounts entering customer payments and making appropriate journal entries. Our accounting supervisor Mr. Long has often remarked about his prompt efficient handling of the duties that were assigned to him. Mr. Davis has contributed greatly to the smooth operation of the entire department.

I am pleased to be able to recommend such a capable young man to you. Do not hesitate to let me know if you should require any additional information about Mr. Davis.

Sincerely yours,

The answers to this exercise appear in the **Instructor's Manual and Key for HOW 7: A Handbook for Office Workers, Seventh Edition.**

Name _____ Date _____

Comma Placement, Introductory Clauses (1-9)

Practice Sentences 9

1. When you see John please ask him to call me.

2. While you were in New York the committee published its findings.

3. Before you leave for Denver will you finish the financial reports?

4. As stated previously we plan to renew our contracts with you next month.

5. Because Mr. Logan wishes to move to Indianapolis he has requested a transfer to our plant there.

6. If so may we count on you to ship the merchandise by November 14?

7. While Ms. Smith was conferring with her attorney her car was stolen.

8. Provided we have an adequate budget you may add one additional person to your staff next year.

9. If you cannot make an appointment at this time please let us know.

10. As explained above this refrigerator has a one-year warranty on all parts and labor.

Check your answers with those given on page 214 before completing the following exercise.

Practice Paragraph 9

When you receive the material please review it carefully and return it to our office within two weeks. If possible note all changes in red. As soon as we receive your corrections we will be able to submit the manuscript to the printer. We hope that if the current production schedule is maintained the book will be released early in March.

Check your answers with those given on page 214 before completing the following exercise.

Reinforcement Letter 9

To: Henry Small

I recommend that we network the microcomputer stations in our Sales Department. Although expensive a network will save money and improve efficiency over a period of time.

If we network our equipment our sales staff will become more productive. They will have access to information processed by other employees. Also they will be able to keep up more easily with the increasing workload in this department. I believe that if the present number of customer orders and inquiries continues we will have to modify update and streamline our current procedures to maintain our reputation for good service. Where possible I myself would be willing to assist the staff in making any necessary changes.

May I have your approval to investigate further the possibility of installing a network to link our microcomputers? As soon as I hear from you I will be able to contact the various equipment vendors for specific price quotations.

*The answers to this exercise appear in the **Instructor's Manual and Key for HOW 7: A Handbook for Office Workers, Seventh Edition**.*

Comma Placement, Introductory Phrases (1-10)

Practice Sentences 10

1. To continue with this project we will need $2 million additional funding.

2. Seeing that John had made a mistake Kate corrected his calculations.

3. After viewing the offices in the Hudson Building Dr. Ruston agreed that they were suitable.

4. Near the top of the new listings you will find the Hills' home.

5. Tired of her usual routine Jan took a three-week vacation.

6. During the next month we must decrease our inventory by at least 30 percent.

7. After the meeting a number of us plan to have dinner together at a nearby restaurant.

8. To be interviewed for this position an applicant must be fully qualified.

9. Until the end of the month no one may take additional vacation time.

10. Encouraged by recent sales increases our buyer has expanded the number of product lines carried by our suburban stores.

Check your answers with those given on page 214 before completing the following exercise.

Practice Paragraph 10

For the past one hundred years our bank has served the needs of the people of Hartford. At the present time we wish to attract more depositors to our institution. To attract new customers to the Bank of Connecticut we have established a premium plan. Hoping that such an incentive will draw a large group of new depositors we have provided a number of gift items to be given away with the opening of new accounts for $1,000 or more.

Check your answers with those given on page 214 before completing the following exercise.

Reinforcement Letter 10

To: Karen Hill

With the purchase of additional computing equipment we will need to compile a series of form letters to answer our routine correspondence. I recommend that when Mr. Black returns from vacation he should be assigned the responsibility of analyzing our previous correspondence and composing a series of form letters to handle routine matters. If possible Mrs. Day should be requested to assist him.

Once the form letters have been compiled they can be stored on the computer. Then when the need for a certain kind of letter arises the secretary may retrieve and personalize the message. This method of answering routine correspondence will save a great deal of time and we will be able to cut costs by eliminating a considerable amount of repetitive typing.

The most prominent office systems magazine *Office Systems and Procedures* has been running a series of articles on word processing programs. In this series the authors describe the many different uses for word processing programs. They also describe the advantages and disadvantages of the various programs marketed by major software manufacturers. Attached are reprints of this series and I hope that you will have an opportunity to read them before our meeting.

I look forward to meeting with you on Monday August 4 to discuss the specific steps we should take to improve our handling of correspondence and reports. As you suggested I will be in your office at 10 a.m.

The answers to this exercise appear in the **Instructor's Manual and Key for HOW 7: A Handbook for Office Workers, Seventh Edition.**

Comma Placement, Nonrestrictive Phrases and Clauses (1-11)

Practice Sentences 11

1. Mr. Sims who has responsibility for reviewing all appeals will make the final decision.

2. Each person who has enrolled at the college will receive a schedule of classes.

3. Her latest article which appeared in last Sunday's local paper was on family budgeting.

4. All students applying for a scholarship must attend the meeting on Wednesday.

5. Your order has already been shipped even though I tried to cancel it.

6. May I have copies of the materials that were distributed at the last meeting.

7. Mr. Davis who has attended many of our seminars is a licensed real estate broker.

8. May I have a copy of our latest financial report which was distributed at the last meeting of department heads.

9. We have decided to hold our conference at the Shadow Oaks Inn regardless of its expensive meals and remote location.

10. Our new company president planning to make major organizational changes first fired three of the top executives.

Check your answers with those given on page 214 before completing the following exercise.

Practice Paragraph 11

The new community library which is located on South Main Street is presently recruiting employees to serve the public during the evening hours. Mr. Davis is looking for staff members who would be willing to work from 5 to 9 p.m. on weekday evenings. He would be pleased to receive your recommendations if you know of any qualified individuals who would be interested in such a position. We would appreciate receiving your recommendations within the next few days since Mr. Davis must hire the evening staff by May 10 before the library opens on May 13.

Check your answers with those given on page 215 before completing the following exercise.

Reinforcement Letter 11

Dear Mr. Little:

Now is the time to obtain the necessary protection for your family in terms of providing them with the life insurance needed by American families today.

We have several insurance plans that may be of interest to you. One of our most popular for young people is our home mortgage insurance. This plan which has been in existence for over forty years provides families with home insurance protection in the form of life insurance.

Our regular life insurance program as you can see from the enclosed brochure has been designed for the family that wishes to receive protection as well as provide for future savings and investment. During the lifetime of the policy it accumulates a cash value which may be withdrawn upon the expiration of the policy or may be used for extended life insurance coverage. Also you may borrow at a low interest rate against the value of your policy should you find it necessary to do so.

Another one of our plans provides term insurance coverage. This plan allows you Mr. Little to purchase the greatest amount of protection for your family during the time that it is most needed. By selecting this plan you will be able to obtain higher benefits at less cost when your family is young and its needs are greater.

Mr. Mills who has been one of our agents for more than ten years would be able to discuss further with you the advantages of our various programs. Please call Mr. Mills at 347-0881 and he will be able to set up an appointment to meet with you.

Sincerely yours,

*The answers to this exercise appear in the **Instructor's Manual and Key for HOW 7: A Handbook for Office Workers, Seventh Edition.***

Comma Placement, Contrasting and Contingent Expressions (1-12)
Comma Placement, Omitted Words (1-13)

Practice Sentences 12

1. The format not the content of the report made it unacceptable.

2. The sooner we receive your completed application forms the sooner we can process you for employment.

3. Tickets will be made available July 1 but only to members of the homeowners' association.

4. The more often you polish this silver the greater luster it will have.

5. I intend to write a full report not just a short memo outlining all the circumstances involved in this transaction.

6. Tom will leave for vacation on June 9; Mary June 15; Ted June 22; and Rosa June 30.

7. Just today we sold six of these advertised living room suites; yesterday three; and the day before two.

8. The Sales Department received 18 copies of the report; the Personnel Department 12; and the other departments 8.

9. Last month we received two orders of supplies; this month only one.

10. Four new expressways will be completed in 1997; three in 1998; two in 1999.

Check your answers with those given on page 215 before completing the following exercise.

Practice Paragraph 12

Last week our agent sold six homes this week just four. Mr. Stevens maintains that our construction site is not appealing to home buyers. His argument is plausible yet weak. Other builders in the area have been more successful in their marketing efforts. Seemingly the more competition Mr. Stevens encounters the more his sales efforts decline.

Check your answers with those given on page 215 before completing the following exercise.

Reinforcement Letter 12

Gentlemen:

We appreciate receiving your order for 12 dozen of our Model 18 frying pan sets.

Because the Model 18 set has been so popular as a summer sale specialty we have not been able to keep up with the demand for this item. We have a number of these sets on hand but not 12 dozen. At the present time we would be able to supply you with 4 dozen.

Mr. Jones who is in charge of our Production Department promises us an additional supply of these pans within the next two weeks. He realizes that the more of these sets that we can manufacture during the next month the more of them we can sell during the summer sales.

The 4 dozen sets on hand can be shipped to you immediately; the remaining 8 dozen by April 18. Please let us know by returning the enclosed card or faxing us your response whether or not you wish us to make this partial shipment. We look forward to hearing from you within the next few days.

Sincerely yours,

*The answers to this exercise appear in the **Instructor's Manual and Key for HOW 7: A Handbook for Office Workers, Seventh Edition.***

Comma Placement, Clarity (1-14)

Practice Sentences 13

1. We have dealt with this company for many many years.

2. When you work work diligently and efficiently.

3. Ever since Mr. Salazar has kept a careful record of his expenses.

4. We were very very disappointed with the final recommendations given by the consultant.

5. The student who cheats cheats only himself or herself.

6. A long time before she had spoken with the company president.

7. Three months before our sales manager had been offered a position by one of the leading manufacturers on the East Coast.

8. Whoever begins begins without our approval.

9. Even before he had never shown any interest in that area.

10. After this time will seem to pass more quickly.

Check your answers with those given on page 215 before completing the following exercise.

Practice Paragraph 13

All the meeting was was a discussion of Mr. Green's plan to move the plant. Mr. Green has presented this same plan many many times. A few weeks before another committee totally rejected his proposal. Ever since he has looked for another group to endorse his ideas.

Check your answers with those given on page 215 before completing the following exercise.

Reinforcement Letter 13

To: Mr. John Allen

We were very disappointed to learn that you will not be able to deliver the main address at our sales conference in January. As you know the staff was extremely impressed with your last speech in Dallas. Ever since many of them have requested that we ask you to conduct the general session in January.

I understand Mr. Allen why you cannot attend our meeting. As national sales manager you must visit other regional sales meetings also. What it is is too great of a demand on one person's time.

We appreciate the many times in the past when you have addressed our Southern Region and we look forward to the time when you will be able to do so again.

*The answers to this exercise appear in the **Instructor's Manual and Key for HOW 7: A Handbook for Office Workers, Seventh Edition**.*

Comma Placement, Short Quotations (1-15)

Practice Sentences 14

1. "Please be sure to remove that sign" said Mr. Grey.

2. "How long" asked Ms. Foster "will it take to repair the machine?"

3. The receptionist answered "no" very sharply and rudely.

4. Mr. Hughes said "Everyone must agree to sign his or her own contract."

5. "Not this time" was the answer given by many of our past donors.

6. "Are you finished" asked Scott "with that ledger?"

7. The witness reaffirmed "That man is the one who stole my car."

8. "Please finish this report by Friday, May 5" said Dr. Ristau.

9. All the union members agreed "to abide by the judgment of the union leaders throughout the negotiations."

10. "Mr. David Brown" said Ms. Burns, the Department of Human Resources head "has been hired for the vacancy in your department."

Check your answers with those given on pages 215–216 before completing the following exercise.

Practice Paragraph 14

Mr. Dallas answered the reporter's question with a simple "yes." His philosophy appeared to be "A bird in hand is worth two in the bush." The reporter then asked "Do you believe this labor problem will be settled within the next week?" Mr. Dallas answered confidently "I believe the terms of the contract will be accepted by a clear majority." "I am sure" added Ms. Hill "that the employees will be especially pleased with the additional insurance benefits offered."

Check your answers with those given on page 216 before completing the following exercise.

Reinforcement Letter 14

Dear Mr. Ryan:

Ask yourself "Did the Wilson Paper Company fill my last order accurately and promptly?" The answer is "yes." Ask yourself again "Did the Wilson Paper Company provide us with the promotional material we requested?" Again you must reply "yes."

We have carried out our part of the bargain Mr. Ryan. We have supplied you with the merchandise you ordered and the brochures you requested. Now in turn won't you be fair with us?

Your account is presently 60 days past due. We have sent you two reminders but have not received a check for $435 to cover our last statement. We can perhaps understand why you have not made payment but we cannot understand why you have not answered our letters. If there is some reason why you cannot make payment at the present time please let us know.

We have asked ourselves "Is this the way Ryan's Stationers has done business in the past?" "Not according to our previous records" our accountant said. So won't you be fair to both your credit record and to us by mailing your check for $435 in the enclosed envelope.

Sincerely yours,

*The answers to this exercise appear in the **Instructor's Manual and Key for HOW 7: A Handbook for Office Workers, Seventh Edition.***

Semicolon Placement, No Conjunction (1-17)

Practice Sentences 15

1. Our company has released a new series of products we feel that the present market will receive these products favorably.

2. Ms. Stephens will file the rewritten reports she wishes to cross-reference some of them.

3. Andrea collated Kim stapled.

4. Place the instructions on the table I will review them later.

5. Steve has begun work on a new project he will be out of the office for the next three weeks.

6. I dusted furniture John cleaned the showcase Mary vacuumed—all just before the store opened.

7. Bill has not finished his sales report for Thursday's meeting he will work late tonight to complete it.

8. We received your application today the committee will make its decision regarding your loan within two weeks.

9. The thief entered he grabbed the jewels he exited swiftly.

10. Sales for July and August hit an all-time low they increased somewhat during September November recorded the highest sales for 1996.

Check your answers with those given on page 216 before completing the following exercise.

Practice Paragraph 15

We need someone to meet with the Atlas Corporation representatives. Please call Mr. Green ask him to be in my office by 10 a.m. tomorrow morning. He knows Piedmont he knows commercial real estate he knows prices. Mr. Green would be my first choice for the job Ms. Jones would be my second choice my final choice would be Mr. Bruce.

Check your answers with those given on page 216 before completing the following exercise.

Reinforcement Letter 15

To: Carol Smith

We are pleased with the results of the new commission plan that was initiated this year we hope that you will endorse it also.

During the past year our sales have increased 40 percent and this increase is reflected in the salaries earned by our staff. As our sales manager stated at last year's stockholders' meeting "By offering our sales force the opportunity for higher salaries through commissions we will be able to increase substantially our sales during the next year."

I believe our sales manager Mr. Black was correct this sales increase appears to be related directly to our placing the staff on a commission basis. We do realize too that our economy has experienced favorable conditions during this past year.

I recommend that we continue our present commission plan it appears to provide the proper incentive for our staff. Please let me know Ms. Smith if you agree with this recommendation.

*The answers to this exercise appear in the **Instructor's Manual and Key for HOW 7: A Handbook for Office Workers, Seventh Edition.***

Semicolon Placement, Conjunction (1-18)

Practice Sentences 16

1. James Hogan who is originally from Nevada has written a book about Las Vegas and he plans to have it translated into several languages.

2. Cliff Lightfoot our supervisor has been ill for several weeks but he plans to return to the office next Wednesday November 19.

3. We have purchased new carpeting and furniture for the office and we expect to have it completely redecorated by the end of this month.

4. We cannot Ms. Baron repair the radio under the terms of the warranty nor can we under the circumstances refund the purchase price.

5. Nevertheless the committee must meet again next Friday but today we will cut short the agenda.

6. Many of our employees live nearby and they often ride bicycles to work.

7. Three of our large moving vans have engine problems but according to the latest information we have received they will be back in service next Monday morning.

8. I believe Ms. Edwards that the contract will expire next week and that it has been scheduled for renewal.

9. You may of course wish to keep your original appointment or you may reschedule it for another time during March.

10. Our last investment program was so successful that it netted a 16 percent return but we cannot guarantee that our next program or any other programs planned for the future will do so well.

Check your answers with those given on page 216 before completing the following exercise.

Practice Paragraph 16

We were pleased to learn Mr. Bell that you have opened a new store on West Main Street and you may be sure that we look forward to establishing a mutually profitable business relationship. Our new line of stationery greeting cards and other paper products should be of interest to you and we will have our salesman in your area Jack Dale phone you for an appointment to view them. He can leave a catalog with you or he can take you personally to our showroom which is located only three miles from your store.

Check your answers with those given on page 217 before completing the following exercise.

Reinforcement Letter 16

Dear Mr. Mason:

We have written you three letters requesting payment of our invoice 187365 for $98.84 but as of the close of business today we have not yet received your check or an explanation why this invoice has not been paid.

During the past year we have appreciated your business we cannot understand though why you have not made payment on our last invoice. You as a businessman realize the importance of maintaining a high credit rating and the damage that nonpayment can do to your credit reputation.

We now find it necessary to place your account in the hands of a collection agency. Save yourself the embarrassment of a damaged credit rating mail your check in the enclosed envelope today. If we receive your payment by Friday May 11 there is still time to avoid legal action.

Sincerely yours,

*The answers to this exercise appear in the **Instructor's Manual and Key for HOW 7: A Handbook for Office Workers, Seventh Edition.***

Semicolon Placement, With Transitional Expressions (1-19)

Practice Sentences 17

1. Our profits have declined this year therefore we are planning a new promotional series.

2. Our supervisor will change next week's schedule however your hours will remain the same.

3. We will not close our store for remodeling on the contrary we will be open longer hours during this time.

4. The foundation built a large new hospital wing consequently we will have additional office space for this community project.

5. All the sixth-grade classes will need new mathematic texts moreover they will need workbooks to accompany them.

6. Send us an outline and two chapters of your proposed textbook then we will let you know if we are able to publish it.

7. Our company no longer manufactures pencil sharpeners however we are enclosing the names and addresses of several companies that do.

8. Mr. Cooper vice president of Western Bank will not be able to attend our meeting consequently we will need to find a replacement speaker.

9. Our computer broke down yesterday for about eight hours thus all our payroll checks will be delayed until tomorrow.

10. Several of our salespersons are being transferred to the Chicago area therefore they will need your assistance in locating homes and apartments.

Check your answers with those given on page 217 before completing the following exercise.

Practice Paragraph 17

Our order for two dozen sets of china arrived yesterday however more than half the sets have broken pieces. These china sets are a featured item for our May sale thus we would appreciate your sending an additional 14 sets to replace the broken ones. Please ship these replacements immediately so that they will arrive in time for our sale.

Check your answers with those given on page 217 before completing the following exercise.

Reinforcement Letter 17

To: Kristin Harris

We have received letters from two of our retailers they are complaining about our service in the Boston area. These retailers have not seen our salesperson for several months therefore their supply of our products has become depleted.

During our special discount sale neither of these retailers was contacted. They were unable to take advantage of our reduced prices consequently they are considering dropping our line unless some specific action is taken.

I have checked into this matter and found that our salesperson in this area has had a declining sales record during the past two years. His supervisor believes that he is not devoting the time necessary to cover all the accounts in his territory in fact his supervisor suspects that this salesperson is in the process of establishing his own business while at the same time retaining his position with our company.

As you know our sales in Boston have been declining and as a result we cannot afford to lose any dealers in this area. I suggest therefore that you contact the two dealers personally and work out a procedure to retain their business. Also I suggest that you work closely with the supervisor in this area to establish a procedure for restoring our sales efforts.

Please let me know the outcome of your actions I am eagerly awaiting your reply.

*The answers to this exercise appear in the **Instructor's Manual and Key for HOW 7: A Handbook for Office Workers, Seventh Edition.***

Semicolon Placement, Series and Enumerations (1-20, 1-21)

Practice Sentences 18

1. Our family has lived in Miami Florida Houston Texas and Portland Oregon.
2. Attending the meeting were David Stevens president North Hills Academy Agnes Moore assistant principal Rhodes School and Vera Caruso director Flintridge Preparatory School.
3. We plan to initiate a new sales campaign for example we will flood the local media with advertisements.
4. Several factors have contributed to this problem namely labor shortages wage increases and frequent strikes.
5. Esther has done all the fact-finding for this case Jim has verified her findings and Paul will take the case into court next Wednesday morning.
6. Members from San Fernando California Phoenix Arizona and Reno Nevada plan to attend the Western Regional meeting.
7. The quiz cards asked the contestants to tell what important events occurred on July 4 1776 October 24 1929 and November 22 1963.
8. We have changed a number of our former procedures for example we no longer approve requisitions in this office.
9. Several of our employees have already exceeded the $1 million mark in real estate sales this year namely Charles Brubaker Dana Walters Phillip Gordon and Lisa Stanzell.
10. Corporate offices will be moved to Dayton Ohio sales territories will be expanded from eight to ten and the position of sales manager will be elevated to vice president.

Check your answers with those given on page 217 before completing the following exercise.

Practice Paragraph 18

Our next student travel tour will include visits to London England Madrid Spain and Frankfurt Germany. Two years ago we received 200 applications for our European tour last year we received nearly 400 and this year we expect over 700 people to apply for this tour. This tour is one of the most popular ones we offer because the Smith Foundation underwrites many of the costs namely hotel accommodations meals and surface transportation.

Check your answers with those given on page 217 before completing the following exercise.

Reinforcement Letter 18

Dear Mr. Williams:

In 1993 our convention was held in Philadelphia Pennsylvania in 1994 it was held in Atlanta Georgia and in 1995 it was held in Dallas Texas. The selection of our 1996 convention site has been narrowed down to three cities namely Los Angeles San Francisco and Denver.

The majority of the planning committee favors Denver however hotel accommodations appear to be more favorable in the other two locations. As soon as the committee has had an opportunity to look into the matter further I will let you know the specific location for the 1996 convention.

For one of the program sessions we have been able to obtain four excellent speakers to serve on a resource panel but before we can publicize the names of our resource panel we must yet receive written confirmation from one of them. So far Ms. Ann Jones vice president of First National Bank Mr. Richard Lee treasurer of Security Savings Federal Bank and Dr. David Long professor of management at Illinois State College have formally accepted our invitation. Our fourth resource person Mr. James Fountain president of Investment Enterprises has tentatively accepted our invitation also.

As you can see plans are well under way for the 1996 convention. We are very close to selecting a site I am sure that we will have a decision within the next two weeks. Many of our speakers have been confirmed and I believe we will be able to provide a tentative program by the end of July. In the meantime if you have any comments or suggestions for the convention committee please let me know.

Sincerely yours,

*The answers to this exercise appear in the **Instructor's Manual and Key for HOW 7: A Handbook for Office Workers, Seventh Edition**.*

Colon Placement, Formally Enumerated or Listed Items (1-23)
Colon Placement, Explanatory Sentences (1-24)

Practice Sentences 19

1. Send me the following supplies bond paper pencils pens and writing pads.

2. Several people called while you were out Marguerite Rodriguez from Atlas Corporation Robert Wong from the Accounting Department Lynne Hale from Thompson Industries and Jerry Horowitz from the home office.

3. Carmen has thoroughly examined this case from every viewpoint she has studied all the evidence gathered by the investigators and the court decisions in similar cases.

4. Included with this statement are bills for January 4 January 8 February 1 and February 7.

5. You may select merchandise from either of these catalogs Spring 1996 or Summer 1996.

6. Employees with the highest rating for the month of February were Naomi Chahinian Bertha Granados and Kelly Crockett.

7. Our buyer ordered the following items last week from your spring line shirts shoes belts skirts and hats.

8. Two of our subsidiaries have shown considerable growth during the last year Belmont Industries and Feldson Manufacturing Company.

9. Four of our products in this series are being discontinued we have had too many difficulties servicing them.

10. You will need to hire 14 temporary employees for our spring sale namely 3 cashiers 5 salespersons and 6 inventory clerks.

Check your answers with those given on pages 217–218 before completing the following exercise.

Practice Paragraph 19

New offices were opened in the following cities last year Albany Billings Dayton and Fresno. We had planned to add additional offices in Portland and San Antonio the high cost of financing has delayed the openings of these offices until next year. Both the planning and development of the new offices have been handled by five persons in our home office Bill Collins Brad Morgan Susan Smith Carol White and David Williams.

Check your answers with those given on page 218 before completing the following exercise.

Reinforcement Letter 19

Dear Mrs. Farmer:

We appreciate receiving your order. As you requested we are shipping the following items immediately

> 1 carton bond copy paper, 8.5" x 11"
>
> 1 carton laser printer paper, 8.5" x 11"
>
> 1 print cartridge for HP LaserJet 4 printer
>
> 2 dozen No. 2 pencils

You may place any future orders by telephone just call our toll-free number (800) 618-4932. Ask for one of the following salespersons Mary Small Bill Green or Ann Smith. If the items you order are in our current catalog they will be sent to you the same day you place your order. On the other hand allow at least ten days for delivery of noncatalog items namely odd-sized printer ribbons adding machine tapes and supplies for equipment manufactured prior to 1990.

We are enclosing a copy of our latest catalog it may be helpful to you in placing future orders. We look forward to doing business with you and toward developing a successful business relationship.

Sincerely yours,

*The answers to this exercise appear in the **Instructor's Manual and Key for HOW 7: A Handbook for Office Workers, Seventh Edition.***

Section 2   Hyphenating and Dividing Words

Compound Adjectives (2-2)

Practice Guide 1

Instructions: Make any necessary corrections in the underlined words in the following sentences. Write your answers in the blank provided at the right of each sentence. If the underlined words are written correctly, write *OK* in the blank line.

1. Please have all applicants for the administrative assistant position take a <u>five minute</u> keyboarding test.   _____

2. All our customer records are <u>up-to-date</u> as of June 30.   _____

3. At the present time our company uses three different <u>word-processing</u> programs.   _____

4. The <u>New York-Miami</u> flight is scheduled twice daily on weekdays.   _____

5. An <u>alarmingly-toxic</u> gas was feared to have been dispersed by the factory's exhaust system.   _____

6. Next month we are scheduled to replace the two <u>slowest-printing</u> printers in our department.   _____

7. The contractor plans to build <u>three and four-bedroom</u> houses on this piece of land.   _____

8. Only <u>Oklahoma-University</u> students were issued tickets to the musical production.   _____

9. All the company's <u>newly-acquired</u> land holdings are in Marin County.   _____

10. Our manager, Mr. Allen, is one of the most <u>kind-hearted</u> people I have ever met.   _____

11. Were you able to obtain a thirty year loan on this property?

12. Most of our <u>charge-account</u> customers have already received advance notice of our July linen sale.   _____

13. Tourists can view the <u>snow white</u> hills against the sky from the floor of the valley.   _____

14. Too many <u>long-winded</u> speakers at this banquet could cause a low attendance at tomorrow night's banquet.   _____

15. My present job is only <u>part time.</u>   _____

16. The First Lady's recent visit to England bolstered <u>British-American</u> relations. _____

17. At least 300 students from our college have applied for <u>interest free</u> loans. _____

18. Three of these programs are <u>government-sponsored</u> and will expire at the end of 1997. _____

19. The daughter Mildred is the <u>least-known</u> member of the prominent Kensington family. _____

20. The <u>air conditioning</u> equipment in our building broke down yesterday. _____

21. Did you show the <u>high and low-selling prices</u> of this stock in the report? _____

22. Please see that these dresses are shipped to our <u>Main-Street</u> store. _____

23. Our sales manager received a <u>well-deserved</u> promotion last week to vice president of sales. _____

24. John's advertising campaigns seem to take on a <u>hit and miss</u> nature. _____

25. Our company bids on both <u>large and small-scale</u> construction projects. _____

26. Be sure to include at least three <u>redeemable-store</u> coupons in the ad. _____

27. Each year our store sponsors a local <u>Little-League</u> team. _____

28. Please use <u>larger-sized</u> poster board for the displays. _____

29. How many <u>basic-accounting</u> classes are being offered this fall? _____

30. This semester we plan to offer several <u>home study</u> courses through our local television station. _____

Check your answers with those given on page 219 before completing the following exercise.

Practice Guide 2

Instructions: Make any necessary corrections in the following paragraphs. Delete any unnecessary hyphens and insert hyphens where they should be placed.

Last week we received several hundred letters from our readers. These letters dealt mostly with the hotly-controversial articles we published on Mexican American citizens in our community. This four week series caused considerable interest among our readers. In fact, it resulted in our receiving a record breaking number of responses.

These articles also comprise the highest-income producing series we have ever published. Circulation rose to a peak-point, one we had not experienced for at least a five year period. Increased circulation was not only in single copy purchases but also in the number of home delivery subscriptions.

The amazingly-large number of responses received from the series was not all one sided. Although some readers may have had a highly-critical response to one part of the article, they often then praised the high quality reporting in another section. Many other readers thought the entire series was thought-provoking and well-written; a few readers did express displeasure with all aspects of the series. As a whole, though, our readers did praise these well-researched and thoroughly-documented pieces of writing. Only the highest level newspaper-reporting techniques were used in these articles.

The long term goals of our newspaper should include more such feature articles that deal with the pulse of our community. These articles should rely on factually based reporting that can withstand controversially-provoked criticism.

*The answers to this exercise appear in the **Instructor's Manual and Key for How 7: A Handbook for Office Workers, Seventh Edition.***

Dividing Words (2-5, 2-6, 2-7, and 2-8)

Practice Guide 3

Instructions: Rewrite the following words or word groups in the blanks provided. Use a diagonal line to indicate where the word or word group may be divided. If it should not be divided, write *ND* in the blank provided.

Ex. *corporation* _____ *cor / pora / tion* _____

1. novelty _____

2. undesirable _____

3. January 14 _____

4. 4397 Halstead Street _____

5. stripped _____

6. letter _____

7. Mary N. Gomez _____

8. responses _____

9. 25 percent _____

10. Columbus, Ohio 43210 _____

11. readers _____

12. critical _____

13. techniques _____

14. San Francisco _____

15. agriculture _____

16. Ms. Darlene Jackson _____

17. 3942 East 21 Street _____

18. December 17, 1996 _____

19. possible _____

20. connection _____

21. brother-in-law   _____

22. thoroughly   _____

23. Massachusetts   _____

24. self-reliance   _____

25. couldn't   _____

Check your answers with those given on page 219 before completing the following exercise.

Practice Guide 4

Instructions: If a word or word group is divided correctly, write *OK* in the blank at the right. However, if the word or word group is divided incorrectly or should not be divided, rewrite the correct answer in the blank. Show word divisions with a diagonal. Follow the illustration shown in the example exercise.

Ex. *be / ginning* _____*begin / ning*_____

1. pos / itive _____

2. congra / tulations _____

3. Dr. Nicholas / R. Montesano _____

4. careful / ly _____

5. March 10, / 1996 _____

6. sup / ply _____

7. 6721 West / 83 Street _____

8. necess / ary _____

9. ob / jective _____

10. gui / dance _____

11. Norcross, Georgia / 30093 _____

12. supervi / sor _____

13. Vir / ginia _____

14. Ms. / Pfirman _____

15. acknow / ledge _____

16. exec / utive _____

17. November / 10 _____

18. Johnson Hard / ware Company _____

19. 18672 / Pontiac Road _____

20. cus / tom _____

21. KRAC- / TV   _____

22. brevi / ty   _____

23. infor / mation   _____

24. 1,350, / 000   _____

25. abbrevia / tion   _____

The answers to this exercise appear in the **Instructor's Manual and Key for How 7: A Handbook for Office Workers, Seventh Edition.**

Section 3   Capitalization

The following materials contain five sets of exercises for the major principles governing the capitalization of nouns. These sets include *Practice Sentences,* a *Practice Paragraph,* and a *Reinforcement Letter.*

Each principle under consideration is labeled by name at the beginning of the exercise series. The section in *HOW* that explains the use of the principle is shown in parentheses.

For *Practice Sentences* use the revision mark for capitalization under each letter to be capitalized; that is, place three short underscores below the letter to be capitalized. Follow the procedures shown in the following example:

Mary richter ordered a model 5879 calculator for each member of the staff in our accounting

department.

For those sentences requiring quotation marks, italics, or underscores, use revision marks to show these marks of punctuation directly on the copy. See the following illustration:

I read with interest your article more vacation for less money that appeared in the march

issue of arizona highways.

Sentences deal only with the principle or principles under consideration. After you have completed each exercise, check your answers on pages 221–222.

Practice Paragraphs illustrate further the capitalization principle or principles under consideration. Use the procedures described for *Practice Sentences* to complete the exercises. Check your answers on pages 221–222.

Reinforcement Letters are cumulative; that is, once a capitalization principle has been covered in a previous exercise, it may appear in the *Reinforcement Letters.* Use the same procedures outlined for the *Practice Sentences* and the *Practice Paragraphs* to edit the *Reinforcement Letters.* Check your answers with your instructor.

Capitalization, Proper Nouns and Adjectives (3-2)

Practice Sentences 1

1. Did you know that dr. chu's new offices are located in the medical arts building?

2. Are there any stores in the promenade shopping mall that sell franciscan china?

3. We will visit the caribbean on the cruise ship the viking queen.

4. During the storm the green tree bridge collapsed into the suwannee river.

5. All our sharp calculators are being replaced by dorsey memocalcs.

6. Did you order caesar salad to accompany the beef stroganoff?

7. Our next convention will be held at the montclair hotel in the city of angels.

8. Miniblinds are a new version of the old-fashioned venetian blinds.

9. This year the dakota county fair will be held in norfolk.

10. All these sketches by john sreveski are done in india ink.

Check your answers with those given on page 221 before completing the following exercise.

Practice Paragraph 1

In april we will meet in the islands to discuss the reorganization of territories in alaska, california, hawaii, oregon, and washington. Reservations have been made for april 7 on a united airlines flight to honolulu. Either american motors or ford motor company cars may be rented from budget car rental for those agents attending the meeting.

Check your answers with those given on page 221 before completing the following exercise.

Reinforcement Letter 1

Dear ms. harris:

We were sorry to learn that you were disappointed with the performance of your travelwell luggage during your recent trip to the far east.

We agree that the locks on your suitcases should not have broken. If you will take the cases and this letter to white's department store, they will repair the locks on your travelwell luggage free of charge.

We are sorry for the inconvenience you have been caused. As a token of our appreciation for your patience and to reaffirm your confidence in travelwell products, we are enclosing a $50 gift certificate that may be used toward your next purchase of any piece of travelwell luggage.

May we suggest you view our newest product, the travel-lite briefcase. Its lightweight feature and durability have made this briefcase one of our most popular products. See it for yourself at white's department store.

sincerely yours,

The answers to this exercise appear in the **Instructor's Manual and Key for HOW 7: A Handbook for Office Workers, Seventh Edition.**

Capitalization, Abbreviations (3-3)
Capitalization, Numbered or Lettered Items (3-4)

Practice Sentences 2

1. Please deliver this c.o.d. order before 2 p.m.

2. The cpa examination will be given at usc next month.

3. Unfortunately, delta flight 82 has been delayed several hours.

4. Enclosed is payment for invoice 578391, which covers all merchandise purchased from you last month.

5. Please refer to page 28 of our current catalog to see an illustration of our model 1738 cassette recorder.

6. I believe the check I issued you, no. 347, was returned by the bank in error.

7. Notice that figure 3 on page 23 illustrates the decline in foreign car sales during the past two years.

8. I believe that paragraph 4 may be deleted from this report.

9. Have you notified the insured that policy no. 6429518-C will lapse in June?

10. Next week we will place our model no. 17 desk on sale.

Check your answers with those given on page 221 before completing the following exercise.

Practice Paragraph 2

The cost of damages resulting from your accident is covered by your policy, no. 846821. However, as stated in section B, paragraph 3, the company will cover medical costs only after the $100 deductible stipulation has been satisfied. If your medical expenses since January 1 have exceeded the deductible amount, please have your doctor fill out form 6B and return it in the enclosed envelope. If you have any questions, call me at 759-6382 any weekday between 9 a.m. and 4 p.m.

Check your answers with those given on page 221 before completing the following exercise.

Reinforcement Letter 2

Dear mrs. rice:

We have made reservations for you on continental flight 980 to new york city on march 18. Your flight will leave denver at 9:30 a.m., mst, and arrive in new york at 3:10 p.m., est. As shown on page 2 of the enclosed brochure, the tour will leave for europe the following day.

Please limit the weight of your luggage to 70 pounds. According to the enclosed policy, no. 48613, your luggage is insured up to $3,000 against loss or damage.

Once you arrive in new york, you will be met at jfk by a representative from our travel agency. She will take you to the wilson hotel where room 422 has been reserved for your overnight stay. Your tour guide will contact you there.

Do have a wonderful stay in europe. We appreciate your allowing us to make the arrangements for you.

sincerely yours,

The answers to this exercise appear in the **Instructor's Manual and Key for HOW 7: A Handbook for Office Workers, Seventh Edition.**

Capitalization, Personal and Professional Titles (3-5)

Practice Sentences 3

1. When does the governor wish to schedule the conference?

2. We have sent all the extra copies of this book to professor Carlos Rodriguez.

3. The announcement was made by Mark Swenson, president of Georgetown Steel.

4. Please submit this application to our vice president, Joshua Wooldridge.

5. We request, professor, that all grade reports be returned by the end of next week.

6. Tomorrow mayor-elect Ann Brown will take office.

7. Each semester Byron Teague, assistant dean of instruction, must visit at least once the classes of all probationary instructors.

8. Only our personnel director was invited to attend the meeting.

9. These orders are to be delivered to lieutenant colonel Bruno Furtado.

10. We hope that Bill Clinton, the president, will accept the key to our city during his visit here.

Check your answers with those given on page 221 before completing the following exercise.

Practice Paragraph 3

The purchasing agents' convention in miami was well attended this year. After a welcoming speech by mayor frank barnes, john lang, the president of williams manufacturing company, spoke on how inflation is affecting the inventories of many companies throughout the country. Also speaking on the same subject was professor roberta holt.

Check your answers with those given on page 222 before completing the following exercise.

Reinforcement Letter 3

Dear mr. ross:

As secretary for councilman john rogers, I, as one of my duties, schedule his appointments. On the day you wish to meet with him, he has an all-day meeting with alice day, auditor for los angeles county. Following his meeting with ms. day, he will fly to washington, d.c., to meet with george davis, senator from florida.

I expect councilman rogers to return on october 15. He is scheduled to arrive at lax on united flight 76 at 9:15 a.m.

I know that as chairperson of his reelection campaign, you are quite eager to meet with him. Would you be able to meet in room 117 of the broadway building at 2 p.m. on october 15? Please call me at 793-9461, ext. 523, to confirm this appointment or to set up a time for another one.

sincerely yours,

*The answers to this exercise appear in the **Instructor's Manual and Key for HOW 7: A Handbook for Office Workers, Seventh Edition.***

Capitalization, Literary or Artistic Works (3-6)
Capitalization, Academic Subjects, Courses, and Degrees (3-7)

Note: The words appearing in brackets are titles of literary or artistic works.

Practice Sentences 4

1. We must purchase the book [a history of the americas] for our history 12 class.

2. Did you know that your subscription to [music world of wonder] will expire with the next issue?

3. Theresa Flores, ph.d., has agreed to teach a conversational spanish class during the next semester.

4. Walt Disney's movie [the lion king] has continued to be a box office success.

5. Make an appointment to see Lisa Gartlan, m.d., for a physical examination.

6. Did you read [a look at teenage life in these united states] that appeared in the April issue of [outlook] magazine?

7. In June Mr. Magnuson will be awarded his master of science degree in engineering.

8. The group sang [singing in the rain] for its last number.

9. We are presently running ads in [the new york times] and [the wall street journal].

10. All the students in our theater arts 23 class went to see [fiddler on the roof].

Check your answers with those given on page 222 before completing the following exercise.

Practice Paragraph 4

   I plan to interview fred case, ph.d., the author of the book [it's easy to make a million dollars]. This interview will be the basis for a feature article that will appear in the [people today] section of the sunday [chronicle]. I am interested to learn whether the ideas outlined in his book came from actual experience, research, or both. I understand, too, that the newly released movie, [how to make a million without really trying], is based on dr. case's book.

Check your answers with those given on page 222 before completing the following exercise.

Reinforcement Letter 4

Dear dr. carnes:

It was a pleasure to meet with you to discuss the editorial problems we encountered with the manuscript for your latest book, [economics for the consumer]. Your production editor, mary jones, agrees with me that all the changes you suggested can be made easily so that the book will be applicable for use in consumer education classes.

As far as publicity for the book is concerned, charles singer, director of advertising, suggested that we advertise the book in [consumer reports], a periodical for teachers of home economics, distributive education, and consumer education.

I am enclosing a copy of an article entitled [the consumer revolt—is it really here?] that appeared in the last issue of [new yorker] magazine. The author's ideas seem to be quite similar to yours, so I thought you might be interested in seeing it.

If I can be of any further editorial help to you, please let me know.

sincerely,

*The answers to this exercise appear in the **Instructor's Manual and Key for HOW 7: A Handbook for Office Workers, Seventh Edition.***

Capitalization, Organizations (3-8)

Practice Sentences 5

1. Please make your tax-deductible check payable to the national fund for the protection of american wildlife.

2. This bill was passed by the senate during its last session. (United States Senate)

3. All personnel employed by the company are ineligible to participate in the contest.

4. These forms must be approved by the accounting department before they can be forwarded to the payroll department.

5. Please ask our advertising department to make the changes shown on the enclosed copy.

6. Yesterday we learned that all county employees will receive an 8 percent pay increase.

7. Contact the department of human resources to assist you in finding a position.

8. Only government employees are eligible to receive this discount.

9. The contracts must be ready for members of the board of directors to sign by June 4.

10. Are you a member of the national council of teachers of english?

Check your answers with those given on page 222 before completing the following exercise.

Practice Paragraph 5

Bill hughes has recently been promoted to head our public relations department. As a former president of both the chamber of commerce and the rotary club, he is well acquainted with many members of the business community. One of his main responsibilities in his new position at fairchild enterprises will be to promote the company among his business contacts.

Check your answers with those given on page 222 before completing the following exercise.

Reinforcement Letter 5

Dear mr. smith:

Thank you for your time and cooperation in helping us conduct the yearly audit of watson corporation. Your accounting department is among the most efficient and well-organized ones I have ever visited.

Hopefully your loan application to the small business administration will be approved. If you would like some advice or assistance in completing the loan application, you may wish to contact john jones, vice president of ryan corporation. He is quite knowledgeable in dealing with sba matters and would be able to answer any questions you may have. I have informed john that you may be calling him.

Please give my regards to your controller, peter swift. We appreciated his efforts during the audit to make our stay at watson corporation a pleasant one.

sincerely yours,

The answers to this exercise appear in the **Instructor's Manual and Key for HOW 7: A Handbook for Office Workers, Seventh Edition.**

Section 4   Numbers

The following materials contain four sets of exercises for several major principles governing the expression of numbers. These sets include *Practice Sentences,* a *Practice Paragraph,* and a *Reinforcement Letter.*

Each principle under consideration is labeled by name at the beginning of the exercise series. The section in *HOW* that explains the use of the principle is shown in parentheses.

For *Practice Sentences* select from the alternatives in parentheses the correct choice for the expression of numbers. Underline your answers. Sentences deal only with the principle under consideration. After you have completed the exercise, check your answers on pages 223–224.

Practice Paragraphs illustrate further the number-usage principle under consideration. From the alternatives given in parentheses, select and underline the correct one. Check your answers on pages 223–224.

Reinforcement Letters are cumulative; that is, once a number-usage principle has been covered in a previous exercise, it may appear in the *Reinforcement Letters.* For the *Reinforcement Letters* select the correct alternative in parentheses and underline your answer. Check your answers with your instructor.

Numbers, General Rules (4-1)

Practice Sentences 1

1. Mrs. Hayes invited (27, twenty-seven) people to her reception.

2. The committee will sponsor (6, six) candidates.

3. (36, Thirty-six) students will attend the competition.

4. Mr. Lucas will hire (10, ten) new clerks.

5. Dr. Francis will lecture on (5, five) symptoms of the common cold.

6. There are (38, thirty-eight) signatures on the roll sheet.

7. (86, Eighty-six) members of the club attended the convention.

8. Ms. Brown has flown (three million; 3 million; 3,000,000) miles since 1991.

9. The department has received (25, twenty-five) applications.

10. There are only (12, twelve) of these radio-stereo combinations left in stock.

Check your answers with those given on page 223 before completing the following exercise.

Practice Paragraph 1

Mr. Wells requested that we send him (seventy-five, 75) copies of our latest catalog. He is conducting (three, 3) separate workshops at Eastern Business College and believes that over (twenty, 20) business teachers will sign up for each course. So that the business teachers can become acquainted with the materials we have available, Mr. Wells would like to give each teacher a copy of our catalog.

Check your answers with those given on page 223 before completing the following exercise.

Reinforcement Letter 1

Gentlemen:

We appreciate your filling our order for (two hundred twenty-five, 225) Johnson serving tables. (Twenty-three, 23) pieces, however, were damaged in transit and cannot be sold in their present condition. Since (two, 2) separate transit companies handled the shipment of the tables, we cannot determine who is responsible for the damage.

We expect that over (two hundred, 200) of our charge account customers will purchase the Johnson tables during our presale, which is scheduled to begin next week. Therefore, we would appreciate your rushing us an additional (twenty-three, 23) tables to replace the ones that were damaged. Also, please let us know what should be done with the damaged merchandise.

Sincerely yours,

*The answers to this exercise appear in the **Instructor's Manual and Key for HOW 7: A Handbook for Office Workers, Seventh Edition.***

Numbers, Related Numbers (4-2)

Practice Sentences 2

1. We have 26 computers, but (3, three) need to be repaired.

2. The number of visitors to this national park has increased from 980,000 last year to (1 million; 1,000,000) this year.

3. We have requested 23 books, 15 workbooks, and (10, ten) teacher's manuals from the publisher.

4. Each of the (11, eleven) applicants gave (4, four) references.

5. Pat found 21 examples of this feature, but only (7, seven) were applicable to our company's needs.

6. There are (382, three hundred eighty-two) active members in this organization, but only (9, nine) are willing to be officers.

7. The prizes—5 television sets, 10 bicycles, and 20 gift certificates—will be awarded during the (2, two) days of our official opening.

8. The produce truck delivered 18 cartons of lettuce, 11 cartons of apples, and (8, eight) cartons of oranges.

9. Our company will manufacture between (1 million; 1,000,000) and (1.5 million; 1,500,000) of these pills.

10. Mrs. Hooper has requested 13 new employees for the (4, four) departments.

Check your answers with those given on page 223 before completing the following exercise.

Practice Paragraph 2

We appreciate your order for (eight, 8) pocket radios, (twenty-two, 22) cassette tape recorders, and (six, 6) portable television sets. At the present time we have only (nine, 9) cassette tape recorders in our Dallas warehouse. We will check with our (three, 3) branch offices and our (two, 2) retail stores to determine whether they have available the remaining (thirteen, 13). In the meantime, we are shipping you (eight, 8) pocket radios, (nine, 9) cassette tape recorders, and (six, 6) portable television sets.

Check your answers with those given on page 223 before completing the following exercise.

Reinforcement Letter 2

Dear Bob:

We are expecting at least (one hundred, 100) people to attend our banquet planned for next Friday. Would you please have the hotel set up (fourteen, 14) circular tables, each one to accommodate (eight, 8) people. Although the total seating capacity will result in (one hundred twelve, 112), I would prefer to have the extra (twelve, 12) seats available in case the attendance rises to this level.

(Ninety-eight, 98) paid reservations have been received so far. I am especially pleased with the enthusiastic response we have received from people who are not members of our organization. In addition to the (seventy-three, 73) reservations received from our membership, we have received (nineteen, 19) reservations from business executives throughout the region and (six, 6) reservations from professors at nearby colleges.

I appreciate your handling the arrangements for the banquet and look forward to seeing you on Friday.

Cordially,

*The answers to this exercise appear in the **Instructor's Manual and Key for HOW 7: A Handbook for Office Workers, Seventh Edition.***

Numbers, Money and Percentages (4-4, 4-5)
Numbers, With Nouns and Abbreviations (4-8)

Practice Sentences 3

1. The new listings may be found on (Page seven, Page 7, page 7).

2. Our insurance agent sent me a rider to (policy 83478, Policy 83478, Policy 83,478) in error.

3. Please refer to the restrictions; (Number three, Number 3, No. 3) is the most important one.

4. (Number 1886, No. 1886) battery chargers are no longer manufactured by our company.

5. The names of all participating dealers are listed in (Paragraph Eight, paragraph eight, paragraph 8, Paragraph 8).

6. The cash register receipt listed items for $1.98, $2.03, $3.01, and ($4, $4.00).

7. Enrollment figures for this year show a (6%, 6 percent, six per cent) increase over last year.

8. These supplies vary in cost from (20 cents, $.20) to $2.35.

9. Our employer has given all workers an (8%, eight percent, 8 percent) pay increase.

10. The new price for these rulers will be (85 cents, eighty-five cents, $.85) each.

11. The wholesale price of these new pencils will be (30 cents, thirty cents, $.30).

12. The highway repairs will cost between $980,000 and ($1 million; $1,000,000).

13. The city council has allotted (four million dollars, $4 million) for the housing project.

14. Ms. Lloyd has a (22%, 22 percent, 22 per cent) interest in the earnings of this company.

15. There has been a (.4, 0.4) percent decrease in the current interest rate since last week.

Check your answers with those given on page 223 before completing the following exercise.

Practice Paragraph 3

A copy of your homeowner's policy, (policy 7832146, Policy 7832146), is enclosed. As you will note on (page 1, Page 1), (line 6, Line 6), the total company liability under this policy cannot exceed (Forty-seven Thousand Dollars; $47,000; $47,000.00). Please submit this year's premium of (One Hundred Sixty-eight Dollars, $168.00, $168). Because increasing costs have forced us to raise our premium rates, this premium reflects an increase of (eight, 8) percent over last year's premium.

Check your answers with those given on page 223 before completing the following exercise.

Reinforcement Letter 3

Dear Mr. Black:

We were sorry to learn that (three, 3) of our (Number 114, number 114, No. 114, no. 114) electric motors arrived in damaged condition. According to our records, we shipped you (Serial Numbers, serial numbers, Serial Nos., serial nos.) 832961, 832962, 832963, and 832964. Would you please let us know the serial numbers of the (three, 3) damaged motors.

We will definitely credit your account for (Six Hundred Thirty Dollars, $630, $630.00) for the damaged motors. Please keep in mind that you are eligible for the (ten, 10) percent discount on the remaining motor. Also, should you wish us to replace the damaged motors, the (ten, 10) percent discount would still be applicable on your reorder.

We were pleased to learn that the (twelve, 12) batteries and the (two, 2) drills arrived in good condition. We are especially proud of the results the (no. 118, No. 118, Number 118, number 118) drill has achieved. Nearly (one hundred, 100) customers have written to tell us of its superiority over other drills on the market.

Please return the damaged electric motors to our Chicago office. If you wish us to replace them, just return the enclosed authorization and we will do so.

Sincerely yours,

*The answers to this exercise appear in the **Instructor's Manual and Key for HOW 7: A Handbook for Office Workers, Seventh Edition.***

Numbers, Weights and Measures (4-6, 4-7)
Numbers, Dates and Periods of Time (4-9 through 4-12)

Practice Sentences 4

1. The Johnsons' new baby weighed (9 pounds 12 ounces; nine pounds, twelve ounces; 9 lbs. 12 oz.).

2. The engineers' report stated that the boulder weighed at least (three, 3) tons.

3. We will celebrate the fifth anniversary of our company on (June 3, June third, June 3rd).

4. Mrs. Lopez will arrive at (6 P.M., 6 p. m., 6 p.m.).

5. Mr. Hodges will trim (8 inches, eight inches, 8") from each edge.

6. The package weighed (4 pounds 2 ounces; 4 pounds, two ounces; 4 lbs. 2 oz.).

7. (October 25, October 25th) has been set as the date for the next board meeting.

8. The orientation meeting was held at (9 o'clock a.m., 9 o'clock in the morning).

9. The flight will leave on the (1st of January, 1 of January, first of January) as scheduled.

10. During the last (18, eighteen) months, we have had two serious fires in our Toledo warehouse.

11. This invoice must be paid within (30, thirty) days to avoid interest charges.

12. In our state no one under (18, eighteen) may work in restaurants that serve alcoholic beverages.

13. Ms. Ige will be (33, thirty-three, thirty three) on her next birthday.

14. Our city will celebrate its (125th, one hundred twenty-fifth) birthday in 1998.

15. Bob Sarafian, (63, sixty-three, sixty three), announced that he plans to take an early retirement at the end of this year.

Check your answers with those given on page 224 before completing the following exercise.

Practice Paragraph 4

When we were in Phoenix from (August 13, August 13th) until (August 24, August 24th), the average high temperature reading was (one hundred sixteen degrees, 116 deg., 116°, 116 degrees). On the (25 of August, 25th of August), the temperature reading dropped to (one hundred ten degrees, 110 deg., 110°, 110 degrees). We did enjoy our (twelve-day, 12-day) vacation but wished our stay had been a cooler one.

Check your answers with those given on page 224 before completing the following exercise.

Reinforcement Letter 4

Dear Mr. and Mrs. Reed:

We know that you will be pleased with your new home. With its (two thousand one hundred; 2,100; 2100) square feet of living space, you will find enjoyment and conveniences that will make it a real pleasure.

As you know, within your unit we have built (sixteen, 16) town houses; at present (nine, 9) of them have been sold. We expect that within the next (eleven, 11) months, the remaining units will be occupied.

We are now in a position to offer you a special furniture value. At prices (thirty, 30) percent below retail value, you may purchase furniture you need for your new home. For example, you may purchase a (model 17, Model 17) Johnson dining room set, which retails for (Eight Hundred Seventy Dollars, $870, $870.00), for only (Six Hundred Dollars, $600, $600.00).

To purchase your new furniture, you need place only a (twenty, 20) percent down payment on your selections. The balance is due (thirty, 30) days after delivery of the furniture, or you may use one of our convenient financing plans. If you are interested in taking advantage of this offer and wish to have one of our decorators call, please return the enclosed postcard.

Sincerely yours,

The answers to this exercise appear in the **Instructor's Manual and Key for HOW 7: A Handbook for Office Workers, Seventh Edition.**

Section 5   Abbreviations and Contractions

Abbreviations (5-1 through 5-12)

Practice Guide 1

Instructions: In the following sentences underline those words or phrases that *may* or *must be* abbreviated in business correspondence. Place the correct form of the abbreviated word or phrase in the blank that appears to the right of each sentence. If no word or phrase in a sentence may be abbreviated, write *OK* in the blank at the right.

Ex.   *One of our leading citizens, <u>Mister</u> Darryl Holtzgang, has consented to donate $1 million for the construction of a new art center.*   _____ *Mr.* _____

1. Please book me on a flight to Chicago that will arrive by 2 p.m., Central Standard Time.   _____

2. Some of the artifacts in this museum date back to the year 900 before Christ.   _____

3. Eleanor Clen, Chartered Life Underwriter, was promoted to head the Claims Department.   _____

4. We have written Senator Lauder several letters about this problem, but so far we have had no response from his office.   _____

5. This show will be broadcast on National Broadcasting Company television next month.   _____

6. A copy of these materials should be sent to Doctor Carol Larson Jones.   _____

7. Only Professor Thomas Propes was unable to accept our invitation.   _____

8. Please purchase three 2-liter containers of 7 Up for the reception.   _____

9. We no longer manufacture our Model Number 1417 cassette recorder.   _____

10. Your order will be sent collect on delivery by next Thursday.   _____

11. The mailing address we have for Ann Knight is 1147 West 118 Street.   _____

12. When you call our office, ask for extension 327.   _____

13. Our imports from the United Kingdom have declined during the past five years.   _____

14. Send these contracts to the client's attorney at 4700 Bell Avenue, Northeast, Portland, Oregon 97206. _____

15. The reception will be given in honor of Brigadier General Retired Foster L. Klein. _____

16. Existing fixtures, carpeting, draperies, and so forth, are included in the price of this condominium. _____

17. The length of all packages must be limited to 36 inches. _____

18. Make your check payable to Yung Yum, Doctor of Medicine. _____

19. Last week Ralph T. Drengson Senior announced that the company would be moving its headquarters to Albuquerque. _____

20. Have you already made arrangements to purchase an International Business Machines Personal System 2 to replace our IBM AT? _____

Check your answers with those given on page 225 before completing the following exercise.

Name _____ Date _____

Instructions: In the following paragraphs some words or word groups that should be written in full are abbreviated; in other cases words or word groups that should be abbreviated are written in their entirety. Please make any necessary corrections: underline the word or word group that is expressed incorrectly and write the correct form directly above it.

Last week Mister Walter Tessier notified us that three universities have already invited Gov. Evans to speak at their commencement ceremonies: UCLA, University of Southern California, and UCSB.

The new chancellor of UCLA, Victor Mallory, Doctor of Philosophy, and the governor's personal friend, Aaron Weiss Junior, both extended invitations to Gov. Evans for the UCLA commencement. This ceremony is scheduled for Thurs., June 2, at 4 P.M. Since the governor will leave New York City at 10 A.M., Eastern Standard Time, he should be able to arrive in Los Angeles in time for the commencement ceremony. Therefore, please phone the chancellor's assistant, Ms. Dixie Slater, at 469-8282, extension 113, to inform her that the governor will accept the university's invitation for June 2.

The University of Southern California and UCSB have scheduled their graduations for the same day—Fri., June 10. Since the invitation from Prof. James Wrigley arrived first, the governor has agreed to accept the invitation from UCSB. Please write Prof. Wrigley at 800 W. College Dr., Santa Barbara, CA 93107, to let him know that the governor can accept his invitation. Also, please send the governor's regrets to Pres. Vern Tuppering at the University of Southern California. Explain carefully the circumstances, and indicate that the lt. governor would be willing to substitute for Gov. Evans.

The answers to this exercise appear in the **Instructor's Manual and Key for How 7: A Handbook for Office Workers, Seventh Edition.**

Contractions (5-13)

Practice Guide 3

Instructions: Make any necessary corrections in the following sentences. If a contraction is written incorrectly, underline it and place the correct form in the blank to the right of the sentence. If a contraction is written correctly, write *OK* in the blank.

Ex.   *We have'nt received your last payment for May.*   _____*haven't*_____

1.   It won't be necessary for you to call in person to order your
     new SMA television set.   _____

2.   I amn't convinced that a strike can be prevented before the
     1st of the year.   _____

3.   This is'nt the same grade of material I ordered from your sales
     representative.   _____

4.   Our company doesn't sell directly to retail customers.   _____

5.   Your one of the youngest students in this class.   _____

6.   Mr. Riley has'nt arrived at work on time once this week.   _____

7.   We'll be sure to credit your account for the full amount.   _____

8.   This movie has not been able to recover it's production costs. _____

9.   Yes, their usually able to meet all production schedules.   _____

10. Who's in charge of ordering the office supplies?   _____

Check your answers with those given on page 225 before completing the following exercise.

Section 6   Literary and Artistic Titles

Practice Guide 1

Instructions: From the answers given below, select the correct one or ones. Write the corresponding letter or letters in the blank provided.

1. Which of the following are correct to express the name of a newspaper?
   a. The Evening Outlook
   b. *The Evening Outlook*
   c. The evening outlook
   d. "The Evening Outlook"
   e. The Evening Outlook

   1. _____

2. How would you express the name of the following song?
   a. A Paradise of Happiness
   b. *A Paradise of Happiness*
   c. A Paradise of Happiness
   d. "A Paradise Of Happiness"
   e. "A Paradise of Happiness"

   2. _____

3. When referring to the appendix of a specific book, how would you express this reference?
   a. *Appendix*
   b. Appendix
   c. "Appendix"
   d. Appendix
   e. appendix

   3. _____

4. According to *HOW,* which of the following parts of speech are not capitalized in titles unless they (a) contain four or more letters or (b) appear as the first or last word?
   a. Nouns, pronouns, verbs
   b. Articles, conjunctions, prepositions
   c. Verbs, prepositions, conjunctions
   d. Interjections, pronouns, conjunctions
   e. Prepositions, verbs, articles

   4. _____

5. Which of the following titles follow correctly the rules of capitalization for literary and artistic works?
   a. In this World of Music
   b. Learning through Proper Study Habits
   c. How to Learn What is Important in Looking for a Job
   d. So you Think You're In?
   e. A Guide to Understanding Literature

   5. _____

6. Which of the following titles follow correctly the rules of capitalization for literary and artistic works?
   a. A Guide to Successful Lawn Care
   b. The Beginning of a New Era is Approaching
   c. What is Word Processing all About?
   d. The Computer Age: an Analysis of Today's Society
   e. Problems of Urban Living

   6. _____

7. How would you express correctly the name of the following chapter in a textbook?
   a. The Office Environment and Its Effect on Performance
   b. "The Office Environment and Its Effect on Performance"
   c. "The Office Environment and its Effect on Performance"
   d. The Office Environment and Its Effect on Performance
   e. *The Office Environment and its Effect on Performance*

   7. _____

8. How would you express correctly the name of the following book?
   a. The World Dictionary Of the German Language
   b. *The World Dictionary of the German Language*
   c. "The World Dictionary of the German Language"
   d. The World Dictionary of the German Language
   e. *The World Dictionary Of the German Language*

   8. _____

9. Which of the following is written correctly to express the names of these famous paintings?
   a. PINK LADY and BLUE BOY
   b. Pink Lady and Blue Boy
   c. "Pink Lady" and "Blue Boy"
   d. Pink Lady and Blue Boy
   e. *Pink Lady* and *Blue Boy*

   9. _____

10. How would you properly express the title of the following unpublished report?
    a. Report on the Reconstruction of the Innercity
    b. Report on the Reconstruction of the Innercity
    c. REPORT ON THE RECONSTRUCTION OF THE INNERCITY
    d. "Report on the Reconstruction of the Innercity"
    e. "Report On The Reconstruction Of The Innercity"

    10. _____

Check your answers with those given on page 227 before completing the following exercise.

Practice Guide 2

Instructions: Proofread the following sentences. In the blank line provided, rewrite the sentence making any necessary changes in *punctuation* and *capitalization.*

1. Professor Schwartz requested the class to read the book a short history of the roman empire by March 21.

   _____

   _____

2. The new newspaper column to and from that appears in the Sunday issue of the springfield tribune has been an unexpected success.

   _____

   _____

3. Did you see the movie an american werewolf in london.

   _____

   _____

4. When will we receive a copy of Professor Coulter's lecture entitled how long can interest rates go up.

   _____

   _____

5. In the preface the author explains how to use the textbook.

   _____

   _____

6. I read with interest your most recent article changing trends in the housing industry that appeared in last month's issue of contractors' world.

   _____

   _____

7. The artist has called this painting mood for a midnight dream.

   _____

   _____

8. His thesis a statistical analysis of two approaches for analyzing consumer responses to newspaper advertising was accepted by the committee last week.

   _____

   _____

9. We hope that our new television series for the love of law will be as great a success as l.a. law.

   _____

   _____

10. When will you revise the pamphlet can you hold a job.

   _____

   _____

11. Be sure to read the chapter economic declines and depressions that appears in the latest edition of our economics textbook modern economic theories and philosophies.

   _____

   _____

12. If you have any difficulty locating the information, be sure to consult the index.

   _____

   _____

13. Last Sunday's sermon it is up to you left the congregation with a challenge.

   _____

   _____

14. When will our class view the movie classic who's afraid of virginia woolf.

   _____

   _____

15. The column brian williams reports no longer appears in our local newspaper the daily news.

   _____

   _____

The answers to this exercise appear in the **Instructor's Manual and Key for How 7: A Handbook for Office Workers, Seventh Edition.**

Section 7   Words Often Misused and Confused

Practice Exercises for Selected Words from *A/An* Through *Aisle/Isle*

Practice Guide 1

Instructions: Select the correct word or a form of the word from each set of word confusions to complete the following sentences. Write your choice in the blank provided.

A/An

1. We have not yet received _____ application from Ms. Harris for this position.

2. Please ask _____ representative of your company to call me.

3. You may wish to discuss this situation with _____ union representative.

4. John will need at least _____ hour to review each file.

5. We must obtain from each patient _____ history of his or her medical conditions and treatments.

A while/Awhile

6. We should receive this merchandise in _____.

7. If you will read _____ each day, your comprehension and speed will improve.

8. _____ ago I sent you information about our new home security system.

9. Although you have not placed an order with us for _____, we still consider you among our preferred customers.

10. Only by resting _____ each afternoon will you be able to regain your strength.

Accede/Exceed

11. Be careful not to _____ your authority.

12. Has management agreed to _____ to the union demands?

13. If this budget is accepted, it will _____ last year's by over 15 percent.

14. We cannot _____ to the landlord's request for a 30 percent rent increase.

15. Your commission on this sale may not _____ $200.

Accept/Except

16. Our restaurant does not _____ dinner reservations on weekends.

17. Everyone in our department _____ Mr. Fielding has requested a computer for his or her work station.

18. For money market checking accounts, all withdrawals are unlimited _____ those made by check.

19. We _____ only cash or major credit cards—VISA, MasterCard, or American Express.

20. Applications for this position will be _____ through June 30.

Access/Excess

21. Because of the floods, all the _____ roads to the city were closed.

22. Building costs for the new offices were in _____ of $3.5 million.

23. Please ship all _____ supplies and materials to our Toledo warehouse.

24. Only the president and executive vice president have _____ to the combination of this safe.

25. All our store locations have easy freeway _____.

Ad/Add

26. How many more salespeople do you plan to _____ to our staff?

27. If you _____ a security system to the building, you will be able to reduce your insurance costs.

28. By placing an _____ in our classified section, you will reach over 27,000 readers.

29. Students may not _____ classes after the second week of the semester.

30. Our last _____ did not attract many new customers.

Adapt/Adept/Adopt

31. Do you believe the manager will _____ our new supervisor's policy recommendations?

32. Too many of our employees do not _____ readily to technological advancements.

33. Fortunately, Nicole is _____ at providing rapid and intelligent responses.

34. Will you be able to _____ this new software to operate on other computers?

35. The instructor's manual, transparency masters, and a computer test bank are all given free of charge to instructors who _____ our book.

Addict/Edict

36. Too many of today's children are television _____.

37. The general's _____ was not well received by the other officers.

38. Only a bare majority of the city council members support this _____.

39. Most of the drug _____ in our clinic are from the local area.

40. Bill manages by _____ rather than soliciting cooperative participation.

Addition/Edition

41. When will the new _____ of this book be available for purchase?

42. We anticipate several new _____ to our staff this year.

43. An _____ to our main dining room has been planned for next year.

44. These artists' prints are available in limited _____ only.

45. Please obtain for me a copy of *The New York Times* morning _____.

Adherence/Adherents

46. _____ to these policies will be strictly enforced.

47. The _____ of his many fans has kept alive the memory of Elvis Presley.

48. Football's many _____ have turned this sport into a multimillion-dollar industry.

49. The governor's _____ were disappointed when he withdrew his name as a contender for the presidential nomination.

50. Your _____ to these regulations is required as long as you occupy this apartment.

Adverse/Averse

51. I am not _____ to experimenting with new ideas and methods to improve communication within our organization.

52. Yesterday's _____ publicity has caused our stock to drop 3 points on the New York Stock Exchange.

53. Our manager appears to be _____ to any suggestions offered by the younger members of the staff.

54. _____ conditions in the building industry have resulted in substantial losses for many subcontractors.

55. The Board of Directors is _____ to expanding our operations at the present time.

Advice/Advise

56. Would you _____ us to contact an attorney for further information?

57. To select the correct courses, you should seek the _____ of a counselor.

58. I appreciate your _____ and will pursue the ideas you shared with me.

59. Upon the _____ of an investment counselor, we have purchased additional shares of CompuTab stock.

60. We _____ you to investigate this company carefully before purchasing any of its stock.

Affect/Effect

61. We have been unable to determine what _____ this advertising campaign has had on sales.

62. Did the unusual summer heat wave _____ your August sales?

63. Do you think the new manager will _____ many changes in our department?

64. How will this merger with General Computer Systems _____ our employees?

65. The changeover from a semester system to a quarter system has had no apparent _____ on enrollment at the college.

Aid/Aide

66. Our representatives are trained to _____ you in the selection of insurance policies that will fit your needs.

67. May we _____ you further by supplying information about our tax-free investments?

68. Please contact my _____ to obtain brochures about the leading companies in the computer industry.

69. Each department in our company has been supplied with a fully stocked first- _____ kit.

70. According to the news report, none of the presidential _____ could be reached for questioning.

Aisle/Isle

71. The carpet in the center _____ of the theater needs repair.

72. Please check the fire regulations to determine how much space must be left between the _____.

73. Catalina is an _____ approximately 23 miles from the Pacific coastline at Long Beach.

74. The _____ of Bermuda is a vacationer's paradise, often equated to Hawaii.

75. Before you take that "walk down the _____," be sure to visit our bridal gown showroom.

Check your answers with those given on pages 229–230 before completing the following exercise.

WORDS OFTEN MISUSED AND CONFUSED

Reinforcement Guide 1

Instructions: Select one of the words (or a form of the word) shown below to complete each of the following sentences.

A/An
A while/Awhile
Accede/Exceed
Accept/Except
Access/Excess

Ad/Add
Adapt/Adept/Adopt
Addict/Edict
Addition/Edition
Adherence/Adherents

Adverse/Averse
Advice/Advise
Affect/Effect
Aid/Aide
Aisle/Isle

1. On the _____ of his doctor, Mr. Reed has requested a three months' leave of absence.

2. According to the last _____ issued by our company president, no employees may park in the customer parking lot.

3. We will _____ applications for enrollment for the next academic year only through March 31.

4. You must separate each row of computer stations with a 42-inch_____.

5. Although I am not _____ to working overtime, I would prefer to work only my regularly assigned hours.

6. This firm specializes in seminars that help staff _____ to technological change and other modifications in the work environment.

7. Please do not permit this year's budget to _____ last year's.

8. Government _____ programs for the elderly have been curbed substantially during the past few years.

9. Strict _____ to outdated policies and procedures has been a major contributor to the company's present financial difficulties.

10. Student records are protected by law, and only certain authorized individuals may have _____ to their contents.

11. Everyone who visits the doctor nowadays expects to wait _____.

12. Large increases in raw material costs will _____ the prices of all our products.

13. This construction company specializes in house _____.

14. We have run this _____ in the *Daily Star* for the last three weeks but still have not found a qualified assistant to replace Ms. Chin.

15. Please have _____ union representative contact me as soon as possible.

16. These new personnel practices are certain to have a(n) _____ effect on employee morale.

17. Fortunately, most of our employees are _____ at upgrading their skills as new versions of word processing, spreadsheet, and database programs are released.

18. We wish it were possible to _____ to your request for an increased wage scale, but conditions within the industry forecast a profit decline during the next six months.

WORDS OFTEN MISUSED AND CONFUSED

19. The new owners of the mall have already begun to _____ a number of changes.

20. Credit card purchases that _____ your account limit will not be approved for payment.

Check your answers with those given on page 230 before completing the following exercise.

Practice Exercises for Selected Words From *Allowed/Aloud* Through *Any Way/Anyway*

Practice Guide 2

Instructions: Select the correct word or a form of the word from each set of word confusions to complete the following sentences. Write your choice in the blank provided.

Allowed/Aloud

1. No minors under 21 years of age are _____ on the premises.

2. Federal law has not _____ major corporations to form industry monopolies since the last century.

3. Please read _____ the president's response to our inquiry.

4. We have always _____ students to petition for graduation until April 30 of the year of graduation.

5. You are requested not to speak _____ during the consultant's presentation.

All ready/Already

6. The materials for these brochures are _____ to be taken to the printer's.

7. We have _____ received over 50 orders as a result of the new advertising campaign initiated last week.

8. As you may _____ know, our division is being merged with another division in the company.

9. Most of our staff has _____ received training on using the spreadsheet aspects of Lotus 1-2-3.

10. We were _____ to interview candidates when Mr. Graham informed us that the position was going to be abolished.

All right/Alright

11. Your test answers were _____.

12. As far as I am concerned, it is _____ for you to begin your vacation on July 15.

13. It is not _____ to extend your lunch hour 15 minutes every day.

14. Our accountant agreed that Lisa's classifying the entries as she had done was _____.

15. Unfortunately, the answers in this test key are not _____.

All together/altogether

16. I believe we can expect _____ nearly 75 participants for this conference.

17. Please gather _____ the reports that have been written regarding this project.

18. If we work _____, we can finish this instructional manual by May 1.

19. We have collected _____ only $10,400 as a result of this charity function.

20. This year's holiday sales are _____ lower than last year's.

Allude/Elude

21. Did the personnel manager _____ to any possible openings in his department?

22. Dora seems to expend more effort to _____ work than she would need to accomplish her job.

23. In your opening address at our national sales meeting, you may wish to _____ to the projected market increase forecast by our sales analysts.

24. Mr. Roberts has managed to _____ answering my questions for the last week.

25. In our annual report please _____ to the technological advancements made by our company during the last year.

Allusion/Delusion/Illusion

26. Although Mr. Smith lives lavishly, his great wealth is a mere _____.

27. Too many people suffer from the _____ that technological advancements will lead to mass unemployment.

28. In order to promote sales, this investment firm created the _____ that all these properties were lakefront lots.

29. Did Mr. Martin make any _____ to our acquiring financial assistance from foreign investors?

30. For this perfume commercial we will want to create an _____ of intrigue and romance.

All ways/Always

31. You have _____ been a prompt-paying customer.

32. Our accountant has _____ notified us of any discrepancies in our accounts.

33. We have tried _____ possible to please you, but you still seem to be dissatisfied with our service.

34. Our employees are _____ paid on the 1st and 15th of each month.

35. Please note that _____ have been explored to expedite the manufacture and delivery of these airplane parts.

Almost/Most

36. _____ everyone in our department has been employed by the company for at least five years.

37. _____ managers expect their employees to arrive at work on time.

38. These sales catalogs have already been sent to _____ all our new customers.

39. We expected that _____ every airline would have already been booked for this date.

40. I did not realize that we had sold _____ all our stock of Hi-Tech video cassettes.

Altar/Alter

41. Please do not _____ any dates on this delivery schedule.

42. We manufacture a variety of artifacts for church _____.

43. As a result of the electrical fire, the _____ was badly damaged.

44. If you wish to _____ your travel plans, please contact our agency rather than the airlines or hotels.

45. Our architect is reluctant to _____ the church plans any further.

Among/Between

46. Please distribute these brochures _____ all our agency managers.

47. There appeared to be major discrepancies _____ the two witnesses' testimonies.

48. The commission is to be divided equally _____ Ann and Phil.

49. We are unable to disclose this information because it is confidential _____ the client and our agent.

50. You may wish to have the office employees discuss this proposal _____ themselves before they make a decision.

Amount/Number

51. A large _____ of people gathered to hear the announcement of who had been awarded the contract.

52. During the next three years, we will reduce the _____ of employees in our Springfield plant.

53. Our company recently sold a large _____ of farm lands to independent growers.

54. Please check the _____ of flour we have in stock.

55. Our store was understaffed to handle adequately the _____ of sales we had yesterday.

Anecdote/Antidote

56. Our manager seems never to miss the opportunity to relate an _____ about one of the employees.

57. Most speakers begin their presentation with an _____.

58. Is there an _____ for lead poisoning?

59. One of our community service seminars for new mothers discusses emergency procedures and _____ for common household poisons.

60. The entire audience was amused by Ms. Green's series of _____ regarding the recent election.

Annual/Annul

61. The agent was able to _____ the contract because it had been prepared incorrectly.

62. The _____ membership fee for the use of your Money-Bonus card is only $30.

63. Our audit is conducted on an _____ basis.

64. If the Board of Directors chooses to _____ this long-established policy, it may alienate a number of stockholders.

65. Both parties were eager to _____ the marriage.

Any one/Anyone

66. Hand a leaflet describing our sale prices to _____ who enters the store.

67. _____ of our salespeople can help you select the refrigerator you will need.

68. Please notify _____ of the instructors in our Word Processing Center if you plan to drop the course.

69. _____ in our Counseling Department can give you this information.

70. We have not yet received an application from _____ who is qualified for the position.

Any time/Anytime

71. _____ you need assistance, please do not hesitate to call on me.

72. Please visit our showroom _____ within the next three weeks to pick up your free calendar appointment book.

73. Our auto body shop can repair your car _____ next week.

74. We cannot divert _____ from this project to review new manuscripts.

75. You may call our toll-free number _____ you need technical assistance with one of our software programs.

Any way/Anyway

76. We are not in a position to finance this project _____.

77. _____ you select to assign these tasks is acceptable to me.

78. We have not yet found _____ to bond these two surfaces permanently.

79. Our supplier cannot in _____ promise a May 1 delivery date.

80. _____, these printer boards are no longer available.

Check your answers with those given on pages 231–232 before completing the following exercise.

Reinforcement Guide 2

Instructions: Select one of the words (or a form of the word) shown below to complete each of the following sentences.

Allowed/Aloud	All ways/Always	Annual/Annul
All ready/Already	Almost/Most	Any one/Anyone
All right/Alright	Altar/Alter	Any time/Anytime
All together/Altogether	Among/Between	Any way/Anyway
Allude/Elude	Amount/Number	
Allusion/Delusion/Illusion	Anecdote/Antidote	

1. We have not yet found _____ to market our products outside the United States.

2. Unfortunately, I do not know an _____ for unmitigated greed and a compelling quest for power.

3. Because of the contract deadline, we have asked _____ everyone on our staff to work overtime next week.

4. Although Mr. Bryce was not selected, our staff was not _____ disappointed in the Board of Director's choice for executive vice president.

5. Please call on us _____ we can be of further service to you.

6. None of us could believe the _____ of errors that appeared in the sales letter written by the new manager.

7. The best way to solve a problem is not _____ readily apparent.

8. If your exchanging desks is _____ with your supervisor, I have no objection.

9. Are you able to recommend _____ for this position?

10. Please distribute these files _____ Peter, Diana, and Chris.

11. The manager's memo left us with the _____ that the in-service classes on computer applications were for supervisory personnel only.

12. Ms. Davis was _____ to leave for the airport when she learned that her flight had been canceled because of the weather.

13. Although neither party wished to _____ the contract, the court ruled the contract was invalid as written.

14. How many times have you been forced to _____ the plans for opening our new branch office?

15. In your progress report you may wish to _____ to the difficulties we have experienced because of the recent snow storms.

16. No children are _____ in the pool area unless accompanied by an adult.

17. Heavy fines were imposed upon the school and its owners for creating the _____ it was an entity of the federal government.

18. Companies that continue to dump waste into the harbor will no longer be able to _____ court action.

19. You may choose _____ of the items illustrated in the brochure as your free gift.

20. Please store this equipment in the closet _____ Room 14 and Room 16.

Check your answers with those given on page 232 before completing the following exercise.

Practice Exercises for Selected Words From *Appraise/Apprise* Through *Born/Borne*

Practice Guide 3

Instructions: Select the correct word or a form of the word from each set of word confusions to complete the following sentences. Write your choice in the blank provided.

Appraise/Apprise

1. Be sure to _____ Ms. Reynolds of any sudden changes in the price of our stock.

2. We have not been _____ of any offers to purchase our company.

3. According to our accountant, the property has been _____ for nearly $75,000 more than the prospective buyers offered.

4. Once you have had an opportunity to _____ the situation, please give us your candid opinion.

5. Have you yet _____ the parents of their daughter's belligerent behavior in the classroom?

As/Like

6. Ms. Harris manages the office _____ a good supervisor should.

7. We are striving to operate this charity boutique _____ a business.

8. You may be certain that we will deliver this order by July 15, just _____ we promised.

9. Although these sunglasses look _____ ours, they were produced and sold illegally by a manufacturing counterfeiter.

10. _____ I said in yesterday's staff meeting, we must create several innovative new toys to remain competitive in this market.

Ascent/Assent

11. The recent _____ of stock market prices has caused even more trading on the New York Stock Exchange.

12. Do you think the Board of Directors will _____ to the president's plan for expanding our operations?

13. Mr. Brooks rapid _____ to executive vice president has caused quite a stir among the other young executives.

14. The plane's _____ to its cruising altitude was hindered by strong head winds.

15. Will management _____ to the union's request for an additional 1 percent pay increase?

Assistance/Assistants

16. Were you able to obtain any additional financial _____?

17. Please ask the receptionist for _____ in completing these forms.

18. Congress recently provided for additional _____ to the elderly and others on fixed income programs.

19. Neither of the doctor's _____ could provide the information we need for this report.

20. If you are unable to attend the meeting, please have one of your _____ substitute for you.

Assure/Ensure/Insure

21. Can you _____ that this project will be completed by September 1?

22. You may wish to _____ your property against other losses besides fire.

23. If you can _____ that I will be able to see Dr. Norris, I will make an appointment for that time.

24. We can _____ you at this time that these dresses will be available in time for holiday purchases.

25. Please allow me to _____ you that we will do all we can to retrieve your stolen goods.

Attendance/Attendants

26. Your poor _____ record was the decisive factor in your dismissal.

27. How many members of the council must be in _____ to comprise a quorum?

28. Each of the bride's _____ will carry a bouquet of delicate pink rosebuds.

29. Before accepting each instructor's _____ roster, please make sure that it has been signed.

30. Please ask one of the ambulance _____ to sign the patient release form.

Bad/Badly

31. I feel _____ that we were unable to locate your lost briefcase.

32. The incumbent was defeated _____ by his young, energetic opponent.

33. I did not realize that I had done so _____ on this examination.

34. Why does the air in this office always smell _____?

35. Marie must certainly feel _____ that she did not receive the promotion to assistant sales manager.

Bail/Bale

36. How many _____ of hay did you order for the horses?

37. This defendant is being held without _____.

38. The judge has agreed to set _____ for our client tomorrow.

39. We cannot even begin to estimate the number of _____ of wheat destroyed by the fire.

40. Please tie all these newspapers in _____ for recycling.

Bare/Bear

41. Many successful businesses have emerged from _____ beginnings.

42. I do not know how much longer XYZ Corporation can _____ these exorbitant losses.

43. We only maintain the _____ minimum balance in our checking account; other liquid assets are deposited in higher interest-earning accounts.

44. The house had been allowed to deteriorate so badly that in many places the _____ wood was exposed.

45. The time allotted enabled me to discuss only the _____ findings of the study.

Base/Bass

46. Do you still play the _____ in our community orchestra?

47. The _____ of this statue is filled with lead.

48. All the fillings in our candies have a chocolate _____.

49. If these conclusions do not stem from a solid _____ of data, then our sales efforts will be unsuccessful.

50. We are still looking for a _____ voice for the company "barber shop quartet."

Beside/Besides

51. Who else _____ Don is entitled to a bonus this month?

52. Place one of these new copyholders _____ each computer.

53. Please move the file cabinet _____ the window in my new office.

54. Several distinguished government officials _____ the mayor were present for the opening session of our convention.

55. You should probably invite other clients _____ those with whom we have had business dealings for over ten years.

Biannual/Biennial

56. Your _____ royalty checks are issued in March and August.

57. The first of this year's _____ reports to stockholders will be issued in February.

58. _____ elections of officers for our organization are held in even-numbered years.

59. These _____ reports must be submitted to the federal government by January 31 and July 31.

60. Unfortunately, this research digest is published only _____; the next issue will not appear for another year.

Billed/Build

61. Have you _____ Ms. Davis for her last order?

62. How many homes has Hodge & Sons been contracted to _____?

63. We plan to _____ our new offices on this site within the next two years.

64. Our plan is to _____ a good relationship with the community before relocating our plant there.

65. Your company has not yet _____ us for the 36 dozen 3 1/2-inch disks we received last January.

Bolder/Boulder

66. Unless we adopt _____ merchandising policies, we will face even greater losses in this tough, competitive market.

67. Traffic was held up for over two hours because a loose _____ had blocked the tunnel entrance.

68. Our new store manager is somewhat _____ than I thought he would be.

69. You should perhaps be _____ in expressing your concerns to the management team.

70. The foundation for this eighteenth-century house is comprised of _____ from the local countryside held together by thin layers of cement.

Born/Borne

71. His efforts have _____ great success within only a few months.

72. Our division in the company has _____ financial losses each quarter for the last two years because of poor management.

73. This industry was _____ scarcely two decades ago.

74. How many children has the patient _____?

75. According to our records, the child was _____ with this heart defect.

Check your answers with those given on pages 233–234 before completing the following exercise.

Reinforcement Guide 3

Instructions: Select one of the words (or a form of the word) shown below to complete each of the following sentences.

Appraise/Apprise	Attendance/Attendants	Beside/Besides
As/Like	Bad/Badly	Biannual/Biennial
Ascent/Assent	Bail/Bale	Billed/Build
Assistance/Assistants	Bare/Bear	Bolder/Boulder
Assure/Ensure/Insure	Base/Bass	Born/Borne

1. The parent company, BTP Enterprises, has _____ the losses of its two subsidiaries for the past five years.

2. Four other dignitaries _____ General Taylor were honored at the banquet.

3. All of us feel _____ that we were unable to complete the project by its initial deadline date.

4. _____ our receptionist told you, we are able to sell our products only to persons with resale licenses.

5. Our _____ conventions are held in odd-numbered years.

6. Please order the feed company to deliver an additional _____ of hay daily.

7. Your account balance has dropped below the _____ minimum to maintain an account free of service charges.

8. This month three of our clients were _____ for services they did not receive.

9. Be sure to _____ our company president of any news events that may affect our industry.

10. The sudden _____ of raw material prices will effect price increases throughout the automobile industry.

11. Without the _____ of you and your staff, we would have had great difficulty publishing this textbook.

12. Unless you _____ the receipt of our order in time for holiday purchases, we will be unable to guarantee its acceptance.

13. Please explain to the manager that his _____ at this meeting is of prime importance.

14. The new shopping center will be located at the _____ of the Flintridge Foothills.

15. Within the last few months, the committee has adopted _____ policies regarding the collection of delinquent accounts.

16. Once you have had an opportunity to _____ the situation in our Chicago plant, please call me directly.

WORDS OFTEN MISUSED AND CONFUSED

109

17. Unless the Board of Directors _____ unanimously to the merger, we will need to take your proposal to the stockholders.

18. To _____ that each payment has been credited to the proper account, please double-check each entry.

19. One sales representative behaved so _____ at the meeting that the sales manager had to ask him to leave.

20. Dividends on this stock are paid _____, once in January and then again in July.

Check your answers with those given on page 234 before completing the following exercise.

Practice Exercises for Selected Words From *Bouillon/Bullion* Through *Coarse/Course*

Practice Guide 4

Instructions: Select the correct word or a form of the word from each set of word confusions to complete the following sentences. Write your choice in the blank provided.

Bouillon/Bullion

1. We are completely out of stock on Hillsdale's _____ cubes.

2. The possession of gold _____ in this country was once illegal.

3. The safe was filled with ingots of gold and silver _____.

4. The addition of chicken _____ instead of boiling water will enhance considerably the flavor of this recipe.

5. We prefer to serve hearty cream soups instead of _____.

Breach/Breech

6. As the months wore on, the _____ between the two partners grew even wider.

7. The judge found difficulty in determining which of the parties had _____ the contract.

8. A crack in the _____ of the gun rendered it useless.

9. Does your client wish to sue ABC Corporation for _____ of contract?

10. Please fill the _____ between the two properties with clean fill dirt.

Callous/Callus

11. Caution our medical personnel not to become _____ in dealing with the needs of our patients.

12. Your _____ attitude toward the children forces us to dismiss you as a teacher's aide.

13. No _____ can form with the protection of our new Syntho-fiber gardening gloves.

14. Police officers soon learn to become _____ to the remarks of irate motorists.

15. My middle finger has developed a _____ from using this punch.

Can/May

16. You _____ mail us your reply in the return envelope.

17. Only members of our personnel staff _____ have access to these employee records.

18. Most of our staff members _____ use word processing, spreadsheet, and database programs.

19. _____ you provide us with this information by May 1?

20. Of course, you _____ borrow these instructions to set up your accounts receivable program.

Canvas/Canvass

21. We are presently out of stock on _____ tents.

22. How many salespeople have been assigned to _____ the Springfield area?

23. Many athletes still prefer to wear _____ tennis shoes rather than leather tennis shoes.

24. Several of the people who work in our real estate office have volunteered to _____ the area.

25. If you were to _____ the shopping malls in this area, perhaps you could determine the buying patterns of residents here.

Capital/Capitol

26. How much _____ will you need to launch this program?

27. The Department of Education is located in Room 450 of the state _____ .

28. Our senior class will visit the _____ in May to tour the city and its surrounding area.

29. In most countries murder is considered to be a _____ crime.

30. When visiting Washington, D.C., you must be sure to visit the _____ to see where Congress convenes.

Carat/Caret/Carrot/Karat

31. One of our customers wishes to purchase a 5-_____ blue topaz pendant for her daughter.

32. We do carry a few chains in 18-_____ gold, but most of our jewelry is 14 _____.

33. When using revision marks, please use a _____ to indicate where letters or words are to be inserted.

34. The customer wishes a piece of _____ cake with whipped cream frosting for dessert.

35. Many pieces of European jewelry are made with 10-_____ gold.

Cease/Seize

36. Our competitors have been ordered by the courts to _____ their false advertising.

37. When did Lenox _____ manufacturing this crystal pattern?

38. Young executives today must _____ every opportunity possible to move ahead, even if promotion means relocating to other parts of the country.

39. Was Drake Industries able to _____ control of Litchfield Petroleum Corporation?

40. We must _____ work on this project until after the rainy season.

Censor/Censure

41. Many countries regularly _____ all mail directed outside their boundaries.

42. Senator Billings was subjected to public _____ once the press disclosed his questionable financial affiliations.

43. The board of education _____ the principal for negligence in not investigating the numerous parent complaints received about this hazardous situation.

44. The _____ have barred this film for television viewing.

45. Not all of the _____ material had been removed from the script before filming.

Census/Senses

46. Which of the _____ are tested by this procedure?

47. Enrollment _____ figures are reported to the state monthly for each of our classes.

48. The latest _____ reports show that the population of our state has increased 5.7 percent during the last decade.

49. At the present time the _____ in this retirement home is 12 persons below capacity.

50. When one of the _____ becomes impaired, patients tell us that others seem to become keener and compensate somewhat for the loss.

Cent/Scent/Sent

51. Although Mr. Wilson is a millionaire, he acts as though he doesn't have a _____ to his name.

52. Last week you were _____ three copies of the signed contract for your files.

53. We are in the process of testing several new _____ for our fall perfume collection.

54. Before completing the arrangements, be sure to inquire if anyone in the wedding party is allergic to the _____ of gardenias.

55. Please do not include _____ amounts in this report; round each figure to the nearest dollar value.

Cereal/Serial

56. The _____ numbers of all our equipment have been recorded on individual cards and entered into our computer database.

57. This new breakfast food is made from 100 percent whole grain _____.

58. When advertising our new high-fiber _____, be sure to mention its crunchiness and tasty cinnamon-apple flavor.

59. Our company will not purchase advertising time on daytime _____ television programs.

60. You may upgrade your version of WordProcessor for only $90 by sending us payment and the _____ number of your current program.

Choose/Chose

61. Most of the employees _____ to receive their bonuses in stock issues.

62. Please _____ your vacation date for this year by April 15.

63. The committee will _____ the final Rose Queen contestants by December 1.

64. Although the manager _____ not to select an assistant at this time, she reserved the right to do so at a later date.

65. You may _____ any color shown in this chart for the exterior of your home.

Cite/Sight/Site

66. Within the next two weeks, we will select a _____ for our new warehouse facility.

67. Please _____ at least two authorities to substantiate your position.

68. Our travel agency can offer you _____-seeing tours in all parts of the world at reasonable prices.

69. The defendant was also _____ for driving without a license.

70. None of the _____ we have seen so far are suitable for the construction of the entertainment center we have in mind.

Coarse/Course

71. You may wish to complete our beginning accounting _____ before taking any other business classes.

72. Before committing themselves to any specific _____ of action, the committee wanted to review more carefully the recommendations of the consultants.

73. The texture of this sand is too _____ for use in the manufacture of ceramic tile.

74. Both homes and luxury condominiums will be built around this new golf _____.

75. During the _____ of the conversation, neither party discussed the financial commitments that would be necessary from each of them.

Check your answers with those given on pages 235–236 before completing the following exercise.

Reinforcement Guide 4

Instructions: Select one of the words (or a form of the word) shown below to complete each of the following sentences.

Bouillon/Bullion
Breach/Breech
Callous/Callus
Can/May
Canvas/Canvass

Capital/Capitol
Carat/Caret/Carrot/Karat
Cease/Seize
Censor/Censure
Census/Senses

Cent/Scent/Sent
Cereal/Serial
Choose/Chose
Cite/Sight/Site
Coarse/Course

1. Be sure to record the _____ numbers of all the bonds in this issue before forwarding them to our New York office.

2. If you refuse to _____ these illegal practices, we will be forced to seek an injunction.

3. You _____ call our toll-free number, (800) 555-3783, any time you need information about current interest rates on the accounts we offer.

4. Too many customers have complained about the _____ grains in our new bran cereal.

5. Most nonallergenic cosmetics have no discernible _____ whatsoever.

6. Proofreaders and editors use a _____ to indicate where insertions should be placed in a document.

7. When elected officials become _____ and indifferent to the needs of their constituents, they should be replaced.

8. The _____ for the new hospital and medical center has not yet been selected.

9. None of these _____ figures support the mayor's claim that business investments in our city have doubled since he has been in office.

10. Our offices are located in Room 450 of the state _____.

11. Within the last few weeks, the _____ between the mayor and several city council members has become apparent to the public.

12. Whom did the Board of Directors _____ to replace our retiring treasurer?

13. Although the governor's personal business activities were not in direct violation of the law, he was _____ by the press for his inability to explain his connection with the Zorga Corporation.

14. Which of our employees has been assigned to _____ the area directly south of Wilshire Boulevard?

15. May I suggest that you select as the first course for the banquet a beef _____.

16. Franchises usually require their participants to invest a substantial amount of _____ before permitting them to operate under their name.

17. To substantiate your proposal, please _____ the names of several companies that have used this plan successfully.

WORDS OFTEN MISUSED AND CONFUSED

18. At the present time most of our housing projects are in the outlying areas adjacent to the Florida state _____.

19. After the convention you may wish to view some of the historic _____ in and around Boston.

20. You will need to _____ this movie substantially for television viewing.

Check your answers with those given on page 236 before completing the following exercise.

Practice Exercises for Selected Words From *Collision/Collusion* Through *Deference/Difference*

Practice Guide 5

Instructions: Select the correct word or a form of the word from each set of word confusions to complete the following sentences. Write your choice in the blank provided.

Collision/Collusion

1. The two executive officers had worked in _____ for several years embezzling funds steadily from their investors.

2. The impact of the _____ was heard over a block away.

3. Although the state official was suspected of being in _____ with the contract awardee, no one could produce sufficient evidence to substantiate the suspicion.

4. You can see from just observing the manager and his assistant, they are on a definite _____ course.

5. The evidence clearly indicated that the security guard was not in _____ with the bank robbers, as they had indicated.

Command/Commend

6. Please _____ Ms. Harris on her excellent sales performance during this quarter.

7. You are to be _____ for having the foresight to install this computer network when the division was reorganized.

8. To operate this computer program, you must first learn a series of _____.

9. The Naval personnel department has assigned a new officer to _____ this ship.

10. Effective managers will always _____ employees under their supervision for a job well done.

Complement/Compliment

11. You may wish to _____ your tempura shrimp entree selection with a mixture of Oriental vegetables.

12. None of the wall decorations in the outer office _____ the rest of the office decor.

13. Please select upholstered chairs to _____ the new gray carpeting that will be installed in our office next week.

14. These calendars will be given to all the conference participants with our _____.

15. Did you remember to _____ the staff on its outstanding production performance this month?

Complementary/Complimentary

16. All of us appreciate your _____ remarks about our products and service.

17. None of the colors selected by the decorator are _____ to the existing walls.

18. The qualifications possessed by Ms. Lee are certainly _____ to those possessed by other members of our staff.

19. To celebrate the opening of our new La Habra store, we will serve _____ coffee and cookies at all our stores on October 1.

20. In general, student evaluations of Mr. Reed have been quite _____.

Confidant/Confident

21. Mr. Burns has been the senator's _____ for many years.

22. When you feel more _____ about your skills, please return to our Department of Human Resources to take the employment test.

23. I am _____ that we will have over 100 registrants for this conference.

24. The information was evidently passed on to the press through the president's assistant and _____.

25. Our sales manager feels _____ that her staff members will reach their quotas by the end of the fourth quarter.

Conscience/Conscious

26. In all good _____, I cannot permit you to take this equipment until we have completed all the safety tests.

27. Are you _____ of the new marketing techniques launched by your toughest competitor?

28. Obviously these publishers have little _____ if they are willing to publish such obscene materials.

29. Two of the entrapped victims were still _____ when the police entered the vault.

30. Are you _____ of the new developments that have occurred with laser surgery within the last five years?

Console/Consul

31. This _____ unit may be purchased in either an oak or a walnut finish.

32. Only standard-sized televisions will fit in these _____.

33. To receive a refund of the value-added tax, you must have the German _____ witness your affidavit that the goods purchased were brought to the United States.

34. Unfortunately, the right side of the _____ was damaged during shipment.

35. Did you invite the _____ to join us for dinner on May 24?

Continual/Continuous

36. Our receptionist's _____ talking irritates a number of our other staff members.

37. We have experienced rainy weather here _____ for the last week.

38. Please place this roll of _____-form paper in the printer.

39. The water had run _____ for three days before the gardeners discovered the leak in the pipe.

40. Customers are _____ complaining about our service in the southwest area of the city.

Cooperation/Corporation

41. We would appreciate your _____ in helping us complete this survey.

42. Several members of our _____ will be attending your seminar on local area networks scheduled to be held in Chicago from April 22 through April 24.

43. Unless we have the _____ of the majority of our employees, this incentive plan will fail.

44. Only through the _____ and hard work of all the committee members were we able to plan and carry through this successful trade convention.

45. Several _____ have expressed an interest in acquiring our product.

Corespondent/Correspondence/Correspondents

46. Who was named as _____ in the divorce case?

47. Would you please direct to my attention all _____ related to this matter.

48. None of our foreign _____ have yet responded with a story from this part of the world.

49. We have received _____ from all over the United States expressing concern over the complexity of the new tax laws.

50. Please have one of the _____ in our Customer Relations Department answer this inquiry.

Corps/Corpse

51. Authorities have still not been able to identify the _____ found yesterday in the desert surrounding Palm Valley.

52. A _____ of reporters flocked around the winning pitcher as he left the dressing room.

53. A recruitment officer from the U.S. Marine _____ will visit our campus next week.

54. The _____ has already been moved to the downtown morgue.

55. A large _____ of government workers has petitioned the governor to reconsider his stand on proposed wage and salary cutbacks.

Council/Counsel

56. Three members of our city _____ are up for reelection this year.

57. I would suggest that you seek _____ from an attorney before taking any further action.

58. The _____ meeting was postponed because a quorum was not present.

59. You should write your city _____ member directly about the problem.

60. Each staff member _____ at least from 12 to 15 students daily.

Credible/Creditable

61. We have received this information from several _____ sources.

62. Your sales record with our company is certainly _____.

63. Mr. Holmes' _____ service record with our organization indicates that he is a likely candidate for promotion.

64. The witness's testimony was hardly _____ in view of the evidence uncovered by the police laboratory.

65. Unless our candidate's statements are viewed as _____ in the public's eye, he will not have any chance to win this election.

Decent/Descent/Dissent

66. Most of the people who live in this area are of Irish _____.

67. At least people in this country are able to earn a _____ wage.

68. _____ among the workers is causing a major problem for our manager.

69. The company's profit picture began its _____ approximately four years ago.

70. Several major stockholders have sensed the _____ between the president and the chairman of the Board of Directors over this issue.

Defer/Differ

71. You may _____ payment of this invoice until the 1st of March.

72. Although I _____ with you on the media we should use, I agree we should increase our advertising efforts.

73. We can no longer _____ calling in these high-interest bonds.

74. All such retirement programs only _____ the payment of taxes until a later date.

75. The candidates seemed to _____ on each issue brought up for discussion.

Deference/Difference

76. We have expanded our business offerings in _____ to the many requests from the community.

77. I find little _____ between the new edition and the previous edition of this text.

WORDS OFTEN MISUSED AND CONFUSED

78. Would you please explain the _____ between analog and digital signals.

79. Have you noticed any _____ in the quality of custodial services within the last month?

80. Most of our imported food products have been grouped according to country of origin in _____ to our customers' preferences.

Check your answers with those given on pages 237–238 before completing the following exercise.

Reinforcement Guide 5

Instructions: Select one of the words (or a form of the word) shown below to complete each of the following sentences.

Collision/Collusion
Command/Commend
Complement/Compliment
Complementary/Complimentary
Confidant/Confident
Conscience/Conscious

Console/Consul
Continual/Continuous
Cooperation/Corporation
Corespondent/Correspondence/
   Correspondents
Corps/Corpse

Council/Counsel
Credible/Creditable
Decent/Descent/
   Dissent
Defer/Differ
Deference/Difference

1. One of the vendors will be serving _____ wine and cheese in the exhibit area from 5 to 7 p.m.

2. If Mr. Smith does not cease his _____ harassment of employees in the Sales Department, we will discontinue selling to him.

3. So far, only three of the _____ members have submitted their reports.

4. We will be subjecting all our new products to more stringent testing procedures in _____ to our customers' demands for higher-quality, longer-lasting electrical appliances.

5. At least two government officials were in _____ with the more than 50 individuals collecting welfare payments fraudulently.

6. Ms. Morris has been the president's assistant and _____ for nearly twenty years.

7. If no one else in the _____ is willing to assume this responsibility, I will gladly do so.

8. The Wilson Agency's many contributions to charitable organizations in the community are _____ to its present management and staff.

9. Be sure to _____ the cafeteria staff on the excellent luncheon it served for our seminar.

10. Are you _____ of the fact that nearly 10 percent of our employees are absent on a regular basis?

11. Please respond to any incoming _____ within three days of its receipt.

12. The recent _____ of interest rates has stimulated real estate sales in general and the home-buying market in particular.

13. For this particular china pattern, a _____ crystal selection would be either Rose Bud or Fontaine.

14. All the shelves in our _____ have mar-proof finishes.

15. Both the defendant and his attorney rushed past the _____ of reporters gathered outside the courtroom door.

16. We will _____ making a decision on this matter until next week.

17. Be sure that your floral selections _____ the tablecloths and the room decor.

18. The air purifiers in our office should run _____—24 hours a day, seven days a week.

19. Upon the advice of legal _____, we have decided not to pursue this case any further.

20. Although his reasons for late payment are always _____ and certainly understandable, we cannot waive the late-payment penalty.

Check your answers with those given on page 238 before completing the following exercise.

Practice Exercises for Selected Words From *Deprecate/Depreciate* Through *Expansive/Expensive*

Practice Guide 6

Instructions: Select the correct word or a form of the word from each set of word confusions to complete the following sentences. Write your choice in the blank provided.

Deprecate/Depreciate

1. Please do not _____ management's attempt to introduce new technologies in our office.

2. Under the new tax laws, investors may still _____ rental properties.

3. The value of some cars _____ more rapidly than the value of others.

4. Employees who continually _____ their coworkers decrease employee morale and increase personnel problems.

5. Property owners in this area are fearful that the proposed airport expansion will _____ their property values.

Desert/Dessert

6. This project will bring water to many barren Arizona _____ areas.

7. Many of our retirement centers have been built in _____ areas surrounding major cities.

8. Our company specializes in creating, packaging, and marketing low-calorie _____.

9. Pumpkin pie is our most popular _____ item during the Halloween-Thanksgiving holiday season.

10. Be sure not to bring the _____ tray to customers' tables until the entree dishes have been cleared.

Device/Devise

11. Can you _____ a plan to prevent employees from copying for personal use company-purchased software packages?

12. Did you _____ an alternate plan for marketing these remote controls in case Video Industries refuses our offer?

13. A _____ within this switch reacts to sound and activates the light switch.

14. Because of snow storms in the East, we must _____ an alternate route to Philadelphia.

15. By attaching this security _____ to expensive clothing, you can reduce your shoplifting losses.

Dew/Do/Due

16. Payments are _____ by the 15th of each month.

17. The early morning _____ lowers visibility and creates potential driving hazards.

18. When _____ you expect the shipments to arrive?

19. The shipment from Hartfield Industries is _____ to arrive within the next three days.

20. You are _____ to have your annual company physical next month.

Disapprove/Disprove

21. Did the zoning commission _____ our proposal?

22. The prosecuting attorney was unable to _____ the witness's testimony.

23. Although we can _____ his alibi, we cannot prove his presence at the scene of the crime.

24. If the insurance company _____ your claim, we will be forced to initiate legal proceedings.

25. The dean will automatically _____ any student petitions that request course waivers for state-mandated requirements.

Disburse/Disperse

26. The crowd began to _____ even before the football game ended.

27. Dividends for these bonds are _____ biannually on June 1 and December 1.

28. You may _____ these blank disks to those employees who use the computer stations.

29. When we entered the room, we found papers from the files _____ throughout the room.

30. We _____ all payroll checks through the Payroll Office.

Done/Dun

31. In order to sell these _____-colored slacks, we will probably need to mark them down considerably.

32. You will need to _____ the people on this list to obtain at least a partial payment on their overdue accounts.

33. We have _____ everything we can to convince these customers to pay their accounts.

34. The white sandy beaches portrayed on the travel brochures turned out in reality to be dirty and _____ colored.

35. If you think we should no longer _____ these customers for payment, then I will turn their accounts over to an agency for collection.

Elicit/Illicit

36. Were you able to _____ any further information from the witnesses?

37. The therapist has still not been able to _____ any verbal responses from the accident victim.

38. The FBI investigated the _____ activities of this company for over six months before making any arrests.

39. Reporters still have been unable to _____ a formal response from any company official.

40. You certainly cannot expect that such _____ maneuvers will be condoned by the Board of Directors.

Emigrate/Immigrate

41. Most of the new residents in our community have _____ from the Far East.

42. How many members of your family have _____ from South America?

43. Several members of our company plan to _____ to Australia to establish an import-export business there.

44. Although most of our employees were born in South Africa, their families originally _____ from England.

45. In what year did you _____ to Canada from Italy?

Eminent/Imminent

46. An _____ Miami physician has recently made major breakthroughs in rehabilitating patients with spinal cord injuries.

47. Were you able to engage an _____ speaker for the opening session of our convention?

48. If these trends continue, a substantial decline in stock market prices is _____.

49. Foreclosure on these apartments is _____ unless the owner can raise sufficient capital elsewhere to make the loan payments.

50. The _____ success of this venture lies in the sales staff's ability to convince homeowners that this device offers low-cost protection.

Envelop/Envelope

51. Please include a self-addressed _____ with your request.

52. An early morning fog often _____ this airport during the winter months and causes delays in scheduled arrivals and departures.

53. Mr. Ross is so _____ in this project that he has neglected his other duties.

54. Layers of pollution usually _____ the area and remain until winds or rain dissipate the layers.

55. All these _____ have been printed with an incorrect return address.

Every day/Everyday

56. _____ we receive at least one complaint about the new salesperson we hired last month.

57. _____ problems such as this one can be handled easily by one of my assistants.

58. _____ for the next week, we will receive at least three shipments from Richfield Industries.

59. For your _____ china pattern, you may wish to look at these less expensive selections.

60. Please be sure to sign out _____ after you finish your shift.

Every one/Everyone

61. _____ in our office will be attending the company holiday party.

62. _____ of the oak consoles was sold by the end of the first day of our sale.

63. Would you please ask _____ to check his or her book bag before entering the bookstore.

64. Almost _____ in the company has been notified of our plans to move the main plant to Springfield.

65. We have not yet been able to interview _____ of the qualified applicants.

Executioner/Executor

66. Whom has Mr. Benson named as _____ of his will?

67. The _____ was unable to locate several expensive paintings that were known to have been in the estate.

68. In many states the death penalty is carried out by a state _____.

69. The defendant is purported to be an _____ for organized crime syndicates on the East Coast.

70. Please have the _____ prepare a list of the decedent's assets for the court.

Expand/Expend

71. Do not _____ any additional effort trying to convince Ms. Hall to remain with the company.

72. Within the next few months, we will _____ our operations to the Canadian provinces.

73. In revising this textbook, you may wish to _____ its offerings to include a chapter on international correspondence formats and standards.

74. As a result, we can _____ no additional funds for advertising during this quarter.

75. As soon as additional funds are available, we will _____ our offerings in computer applications courses.

Expansive/Expensive

76. _____ wastelands are dominant in this area of the country.

77. The cost of implementing your proposal is more _____ than we had anticipated.

78. Many _____ paintings were damaged by the fire.

79. Only _____ gourmet foods are stocked in this section of the store.

80. An _____ industrial center will be developed on this acreage.

Check your answers with those given on pages 239–240 before completing the following exercise.

Reinforcement Guide 6

Instructions: Select one of the words (or a form of the word) shown below to complete each of the following sentences.

Deprecate/Depreciate   Done/Dun   Every one/Everyone
Desert/Dessert   Elicit/Illicit   Executioner/Executor
Device/Devise   Emigrate/Immigrate   Expand/Expend
Dew/Do/Due   Eminent/Imminent   Expansive/Expensive
Disapprove/Disprove   Envelop/Envelope
Disburse/Disperse   Every day/Everyday

1. Please give _____ at the meeting a copy of this report.

2. Several members of our staff have _____ from the Philippines.

3. If the hospital administrator _____ our budget request for an additional therapist, we will need to reduce our out-patient caseload.

4. Employees who continually _____ their supervisors are usually substandard workers who are unable to adjust to the work environment.

5. The court date for your official appointment as _____ of the estate has been set for August 21.

6. The _____ threat of further flood damage has caused the area to be evacuated.

7. Did you hire an agency to _____ these fliers throughout the neighborhood?

8. For the board meeting next week, we plan to serve coffee and _____.

9. Do not _____ any additional time or effort attempting to locate these misplaced files.

10. All the employees stood in shock as they watched the flames _____ the warehouse.

11. The only distasteful part of this job is having to _____ slow-paying customers.

12. As soon as you _____ a new method for handling these payment coupons, please let me know.

13. To accommodate all the buildings in the architect's renderings, we will need a more _____ area than the site offered by your company.

14. Our receptionist has been late to work _____ this week.

15. Were you able to _____ any further information about ITV's new operating system from any of our customers?

16. These payroll reports are _____ quarterly and must be submitted on time.

17. According to the decedent's will, his real estate holdings are to be sold and the proceeds _____ to the charities named.

18. When did you _____ to the United States?

19. _____ physicists from all over the world will gather for this convention.

20. Our editor in chief cannot allow the _____ problems of operating the division occupy the major part of her time.

Check your answers with those given on page 240 before completing the following exercise.

WORDS OFTEN MISUSED AND CONFUSED

Practice Exercises for Selected Words From *Explicit/Implicit* Through *Former/Latter*

Practice Guide 7

Instructions: Select the correct word or a form of the word from each set of word confusions to complete the following sentences. Write your choice in the blank provided.

Explicit/Implicit

1. The fact that you are qualified for the job is _____ in your being offered employment by three major corporations.

2. These instructions state _____, "Do not spray the saline solution directly into the eye."

3. _____ instructions for assembling these computers have been placed in each carton.

4. You are _____ consenting to these price increases by uttering no objections.

5. Your _____ directions were very easy to follow.

Extant/Extent

6. We have still been unable to determine the _____ of the damage caused by the warehouse fire.

7. All our _____ construction projects have been financed fully by various banks.

8. Some of the original buildings occupied by our company at the turn of the century are _____.

9. To what _____ do you foresee our involvement in this political campaign?

10. Most of the _____ earliest automobiles are owned by museums.

Facetious/Factious

11. Since the president lacks a sense of humor, please refrain from making any _____ remarks during his presentation.

12. Although seemingly _____, his statement bordered on sarcasm.

13. The new manager's _____ temperament can only result in continual dissension.

14. Our declining profit picture during the last year can be attributed directly to the Board of Directors' _____ handling of company affairs.

15. Our manager is well-known for his _____ comments and dry sense of humor.

Factitious/Fictitious

16. Is this company still operating under a _____ business name?

17. The salesperson's _____ mannerisms and responses caused me to lose confidence in this potential real estate investment.

18. Too many employees in this hospital have only a _____ concern for the welfare of the patients.

19. According to the author, all the characters in his new book, *The White House Controversy*, are _____.

20. The court has already established that the defendant has used at least three _____ names.

Fair/Fare

21. We can expect to see substantial _____ increases on all airlines for December.

22. The county _____ is held annually during the latter part of September.

23. Our firm has been engaged to ensure a _____ distribution of assets to all the creditors of record at the time of the bankruptcy.

24. We expect our employees to do more than just a _____ job.

25. How well did you _____ in the forensics competition?

Farther/Further

26. If we can assist you any _____, please let us know.

27. Your office is _____ from the airport than mine.

28. Once I have had an opportunity to look into this matter _____, I will contact you again.

29. The _____ you live from campus, the better chance you will have of obtaining on-campus university housing.

30. Had you read _____, you would have seen the paragraph in the contract that grants the publisher full editing authority.

Feat/Fete

31. The banquet to _____ our retiring football coach will be held on May 22.

32. The _____ accomplished by Rafer Johnson in the 1960 Olympics have yet to be exceeded—or even duplicated.

33. Such a _____ of daring and courage could have been accomplished by only a few.

34. How many people do you expect will attend this _____ to celebrate our company's one hundredth anniversary?

35. After the election the new mayor was _____ by his many supporters and friends.

Fewer/Less

36. Because _____ than 15 people had registered for the class, the dean canceled it.

37. We received _____ responses to this advertisement than we had anticipated.

38. Please do not accept deposits that are _____ than half the total order.

39. Only orders containing ten or _____ items may be processed through our fast-service checkout line.

40. _____ than 30 percent of our investors have responded to the questionnaire.

Finally/Finely

41. We were _____ able to contact all the sweepstake winners.

42. These walnut pieces are too coarse to be graded as "_____ chopped."

43. Our _____ trained athletes should perform well in the next Olympics.

44. When we _____ received the information from our central office, it arrived too late to assist us in making a decision.

45. We _____ raised enough capital to purchase the building site on Washington Boulevard.

Flagrant/Fragrant

46. The board of education could not even begin to defend the _____ actions of its newly appointed superintendent.

47. How could the governor have made such a _____ error?

48. Do not send highly _____ flowers to persons who suffer from allergies.

49. The newspapers were filled with stories of the _____ crimes committed by the hired assassins.

50. Our new line of _____ spices has achieved popularity as gift items for this holiday season.

Flair/Flare

51. Our new office manager has a _____ for color coordination and interior design.

52. Your _____ for calming irate customers will bring you much success in sales.

53. If Mr. Dodd allows his temper to _____ each time he encounters an adverse situation, he will certainly not be considered for promotion.

54. Be sure to get sufficient rest so that your laryngitis does not _____ up again.

55. _____ skirts are popular again this season.

Flaunt/Flout

56. People who _____ their wealth are usually not well liked by others.

57. American tourists should not _____ foreign customs when visiting other countries.

58. By _____ his attorney's advice, the defendant was sentenced to an even longer term.

59. Those construction workers who _____ the safety rules and procedures on this project will be dismissed immediately.

60. Bob distracts and embarrasses many members of the staff by continually _____ his vices.

Flew/Flu/Flue

61. Please call a service person to repair the chimney _____ in Suite 1420-22.

62. Most of our employees have had the _____ at least one time or another this winter.

63. Please instruct the hotel guests to open the _____ before using the fireplace.

64. The executive staff _____ first-class to New York, but all other company personnel were given tourist class seating.

65. Do many of the elderly residents in this retirement home request _____ shots each season?

Formally/Formerly

66. The committee's selection will be announced _____ on July 14.

67. Ms. Greeley was _____ associated with Stanfield Industries.

68. Yes, we _____ were the primary distributors for this product line on the East Coast.

69. Our new product line will be _____ introduced at the International Computer Show in Chicago on March 25.

70. For this event all ladies and gentlemen must be _____ attired.

Former/Latter

71. Please send a copy of this report to the _____ company president.

72. From among your present and _____ instructors, please list three references.

73. Our inventory must be completed during the _____ part of January.

74. Mr. Thompson's _____ proposal seems to be more practicable than this new one.

WORDS OFTEN MISUSED AND CONFUSED

75. Both John Dixon, manager of our Toledo branch, and Brett Johnson, manager of our Louisville branch, applied for the position; but Brett, the _____, is more qualified.

Check your answers with those given on pages 241–242 before completing the following exercise.

Reinforcement Guide 7

Instructions: Select one of the words (or a form of the word) shown below to complete each of the following sentences.

Explicit/Implicit	Farther/Further	Flair/Flare
Extant/Extent	Feat/Fete	Flaunt/Flout
Facetious/Factious	Fewer/Less	Flew/Flu/Flue
Factitious/Fictitious	Finally/Finely	Formally/Formerly
Fair/Fare	Flagrant/Fragrant	Former/Latter

1. The Northridge Chamber of Commerce will honor its _____ presidents at the next meeting.

2. Any _____ memorabilia belonging to Elvis Presley has already been sold at public auction.

3. All funds raised by this telethon will be donated to _____ cancer research.

4. A large _____ is planned for the benefit of the proposed new hospital wing.

5. The hillside fires, which were thought to be under control yesterday evening, _____ out of control this morning.

6. Any child who continually _____ the school rules will be suspended.

7. An error in the advertising copy has caused a _____ demand for our 60-minute video cassettes.

8. By not objecting to the proposal, the national sales manager gave us her _____ consent to follow through with this new marketing plan.

9. Please telephone our travel agent and request information regarding _____ to Atlanta for the week of November 10.

10. Ms. Butler has a _____ for solving usage problems with our word processing, spreadsheet, and database programs.

11. If _____ than ten people sign up for the seminar on August 10, we will need to reschedule it after the vacation period.

12. Our company was _____ a subsidiary of Walton Industries.

13. _____ deviations from company policy such as these will surely cost the manager his job.

14. To meet the deadline date on this project, our department worked together like a _____ tuned orchestra.

15. If you continue to foster _____ behavior among the office staff, we will be forced to hire a new office manager.

16. Because the _____ had inadvertently been closed, smoke from the fireplace filled the restaurant and set off the fire alarm.

17. Please supply us with _____ instructions for cleaning these tape decks.

18. Minors who present _____ identification are in violation of the law.

19. The speaker's presentation was filled with _____ remarks and humorous stories.

20. Although Don was elated that he had been chosen for the position, he should not have _____ his success in front of the others who had applied.

Check your answers with those given on page 242 before completing the following exercise.

Practice Exercises for Selected Words From *Forth/Fourth* Through *Imply/Infer*

Practice Guide 8

Instructions: Select the correct word or a form of the word from each set of word confusions to complete the following sentences. Write your choice in the blank provided.

Forth/Fourth

1. Amalgamated Enterprises represents the _____ contract we have received this month.

2. Please do not hesitate to set _____ any ideas you may have regarding this proposal.

3. Nearly one _____ of our sales staff has already reached its quota for the year.

4. You may need to reword for clarity the _____ question in this survey instrument.

5. Before we begin writing the grant proposal, we need to set _____ goals and objectives.

Good/Well

6. The last group of candidates did very _____ on this promotional examination.

7. Since I did not feel _____ yesterday, I left the office early.

8. If employees do not feel _____ about themselves and their work, they will become disgruntled.

9. At the present time economic forecasts for our industry look _____.

10. Unfortunately, our basketball team did not do _____ enough in the preliminaries to qualify for the finals.

Grate/Great

11. I hope that the new mayor and his staff will meet the _____ expectations of our citizenry.

12. Please use a solid cover instead of a _____ for this open shaft.

13. You may wish to _____ all these smaller, unusable pieces into wood shavings.

14. Do his rude manners and loud voice _____ on you too?

15. A number of _____ American leaders have stayed in this hotel during the last century.

Guarantee/Guaranty

16. Once your parents have signed the _____, we will begin processing the loan papers.

17. This one-year _____ includes parts and labor.

18. If you can _____ that the building will be ready for occupancy by October 15, we will sign the contract with your firm.

19. To lease this apartment for your mother, you must complete and sign this _____ for the rental payments.

20. For how long do you _____ your work?

He/Him/Himself

21. Although the choice is only between you and _____, the committee has still not made a decision.

22. We all suspected that the new president would be _____.

23. Since Bill agreed to write the report _____, the other committee members volunteered to assist him with editing and proofreading it.

24. The person selected for this top administrative post was not _____.

25. Please ask Marie, Chris, or_____ to assist you with compiling the sales figures for this month.

Hear/Here

26. Return the form _____ when you have completed it.

27. Were you _____ when the manager requested us to join her for a brief meeting after the store closes?

28. None of us in the back row were able to _____ the general session speaker.

29. If you _____ of any job openings in this area, please let me know.

30. These tests are administered only _____ in the laboratory.

Her/Herself/She

31. Donna _____ was not sure whether or not she had set the alarm before leaving the office.

32. If Bob or _____ request this confidential information, please give it to either one of them.

33. As soon as we receive the signed contracts, I will assign either my assistant or _____ to set up the account.

34. The most qualified person for this position is obviously _____.

35. If I were _____, I would request a leave of absence instead of resigning outright.

WORDS OFTEN MISUSED AND CONFUSED

Hew/Hue

36. Most of the objects in our gallery are _____ from wood or stone.

37. This fabric contains most of the _____ of the rainbow.

38. Musicians and music fans from every _____ should be attracted to this exhibition.

39. We must _____ down this tree before its roots penetrate the retaining wall.

40. We have not yet been able to locate a silk with the particular pinkish _____ we need.

Hoard/Horde

41. _____ of locusts destroyed the crops in this region last season.

42. A _____ of fans gathered around the star as he attempted to leave the stadium.

43. Please request employees not to _____ quantities of blank floppy disks in their desks.

44. Rumors of shortages can cause consumers to _____ goods, which in turn can cause factitious demands for these products.

45. The officers seized the smugglers' _____ of contraband.

Hole/Whole

46. Our doughnut-_____ sales are almost one third of our doughnut sales.

47. Honey Baked Hams are sold _____ or in halves only.

48. We will not make any decisions until we have heard the _____ story.

49. If tenants drill _____ in the walls, they are responsible for the costs to patch and repaint the walls when they move.

50. The _____ conference will be devoted to research and research methods.

Holy/Wholly

51. I am not _____ convinced that this proposal should be financed to its maximum.

52. A number of _____ relics were destroyed in the fire.

53. All members of the committee _____ support your idea.

54. The new stock issue was purchased _____ by small investors.

55. Although you may not _____ agree with them, I am sure you understand the reasons for our decision.

Human/Humane

56. This diagram illustrates the flow of blood through the _____ heart.

57. These new mannequins look almost _____.

58. _____ people are considerate of animals.

59. Our editor has requested us to submit more _____-interest stories for the Sunday edition.

60. The American prison system advocates the _____ treatment of inmates.

Hypercritical/Hypocritical

61. _____ and demanding supervisors generally experience a high degree of personnel turnover in their units.

62. Your inflexible and _____ view of office technologies will certainly cost you your job.

63. The press soon labeled this "would-be" council member _____ after citing several glaring inconsistencies in speeches to different community groups.

64. The Board of Directors was in my estimation _____ of the president's reorganization plan.

65. Too many politicians are _____; they tell the voters what they want to hear before the election but do as they please after the election.

I/Me/Myself

66. You may submit your reports to either Jan or _____.

67. It was _____ who conducted the in-service training program last month.

68. David, Lisa, and _____ are responsible for conducting this survey of consumer preferences.

69. Please ask the branch managers to fill out and return these questionnaires to Ms. Reynolds or _____.

70. The only person who has access to these files in our unit is _____.

Ideal/Idle/Idol

71. Our receptionist appears to have too much _____ time.

72. In just three years this pitcher has become a baseball _____ and made millions of dollars.

73. The site on the corner of Fourth Street and Jefferson Avenue is an _____ location for our proposed new branch office.

74. Our mainframe computer has already lain _____ for nearly seven hours.

75. Although none of these solutions is _____, we must select one.

Imply/Infer

76. To others, silence may _____ consent.

77. I did not mean to _____ that your statement was incorrect.

78. We _____ from the principal's statement that he knew who had broken the window.

79. The results of this survey _____ that our present computer installation is not paying for itself.

80. The newspaper article _____ that several computer software companies would be making significant announcements this month.

Check your answers with those given on pages 243–244 before completing the following exercise.

Reinforcement Guide 8

Instructions: Select one of the words (or a form of the word) shown below to complete each of the following sentences.

Forth/Fourth	Her/Herself/She	Hypercritical/Hypocritical
Good/Well	Hew/Hue	I/Me/Myself
Grate/Great	Hoard/Horde	Ideal/Idle/Idol
Guarantee/Guaranty	Hole/Whole	Imply/Infer
He/Him/Himself	Holy/Wholly	
Hear/Here	Human/Humane	

1. Because she is consistently _____ of others' efforts, most members of the staff refuse to work closely with her.

2. Many people today still _____ large sums of cash instead of depositing them in savings accounts.

3. The winner of our monthly sales contest was _____, David Larson.

4. The prosecution's surprise witness seemed to come _____ from nowhere.

5. If you will return the completed application to either Ms. Davis or _____, we will process it without any further delays.

6. Once we receive the _____ shipment, we will send you full payment for Invoice 874659H.

7. As soon as we _____ from the lender, we will notify you.

8. This student does not read _____ enough to work at grade level.

9. Your administrative assistant appears to have too much _____ time on his hands.

10. Based on the outcome of the vote, we can only assume that the board was not _____ convinced that our proposal is the solution to this problem.

11. Mary requested the respondents to return the questionnaire to _____ .

12. Mark down all our fireplace _____ 40 percent for this weekend sale.

13. We have no other choice but to _____ from the number of complaint letters we have received that the service provided by your branch office needs to be improved.

14. Our society has dedicated itself to alleviateing _____ suffering throughout the world.

15. Most of the stones used to build this home were _____ from giant rocks in the adjacent mountain area.

16. Once your parent company has signed the _____, we will issue a check for the amount of the loan.

17. I did not intend to _____ that your products were inferior to those of your competitors.

18. Politicians are often accused of being _____ when they do not fulfill their campaign promises.

19. Most of our students do _____ on college entrance examinations.

20. As I left the court, a _____ of reporters surrounded me.

Check your answers with those given on page 244 before completing the following exercise.

Practice Exercises for Selected Words From *Incidence/Incidents* Through *Liable/Libel*

Practice Guide 9

Instructions: Select the correct word or a form of the word from each set of word confusions to complete the following sentences. Write your choice in the blank provided.

Incidence/Incidents

1. Have you reported any of these _____ to the police?

2. We have yet to have any _____ requiring us to use this feature of your software program.

3. Because such an _____ in our company would be highly unlikely, your proposal does not suit our needs.

4. All the _____ you describe occurred without my knowledge or the knowledge of any other member of the administrative staff.

5. Too few _____ require our using teleconferencing for us to invest in our own studio.

Incite/Insight

6. Perhaps the new president will _____ more members to participate in our association's activities and projects.

7. A small group of agitators _____ the union members to strike.

8. The Board of Directors is looking for a chief executive officer with _____ and experience in human relations.

9. Without any _____ into the internal workings of the company, I cannot predict how successful it might become.

10. Do your political science courses _____ students to become more politically active?

Indigenous/Indigent/Indignant

11. Pineapples are _____ to Hawaii and constitute one of its major products.

12. Although his beginnings were _____, Mr. Simon has risen to become one of America's financial giants.

13. _____ accused of crimes in this state may secure the services of a public defender.

14. Your _____ attitude seems unjustified in this situation.

15. This kind of generosity and concern is _____ of her character and personality.

Ingenious/Ingenuous

16. _____ ideas such as this one come only once in a lifetime.

17. According to the news reports, the _____ boy was able to invade the computer files of many major corporations throughout the state.

18. Our _____ receptionist would never be suspicious of anything our clients tell her.

19. This makeshift car door opener formed from a wire coat hangar is an _____ device.

20. The defendant seemed to give an _____ account of his acts, concealing nothing.

Interstate/Intrastate

21. Since our food chain is _____, we are subject only to Colorado statutes.

22. Our _____ activities are primarily among Texas, Oklahoma, and New Mexico.

23. Commercial trucks traveling _____ must be licensed by all states in which their companies have offices.

24. The federal government regulates _____ commerce.

25. Our licensing program does not have reciprocity with any other state; therefore, you may practice _____ only.

Its/It's

26. If _____ too late for us to purchase tickets for the August 12 performance, please see if you can obtain tickets for August 19 or August 26.

27. We have been forced to close our Westchester branch temporarily because _____ new location is not yet ready for occupancy.

28. The building has been closed down by the fire department because _____ unsafe for occupancy.

29. The union has requested all _____ members to approve the new contract.

30. When will the chamber of commerce have _____ annual holiday party for needy children?

Later/Latter

31. All the electrical work in this housing tract must be completed by the _____ part of April.

32. Unfortunately, we are unable to schedule a _____ appointment for you.

33. Is this class offered at a _____ time also?

34. Her _____ design for the building facade is more creative and eye-appealing.

35. Neither of his proposals was accepted by the committee, although the _____ one showed more promise.

Lay/Lie

36. Please request the patient to _____ down on the examination table.

37. Our computer system has _____ idle for nearly 24 hours.

38. The victim _____ in his car for over two hours before the highway patrol discovered the wreckage in the gully beside the highway.

39. Why have these files been _____ on my desk for the last week?

40. The new shopping center _____ at the base of the Verdugo Foothills.

Lean/Lien

41. Our restaurant serves only _____ meats and fresh vegetables.

42. I believe the Board of Directors _____ toward divesting the company's interests in all oil stocks.

43. Several subcontractors have already placed _____ against the property.

44. Do not _____ the folding chairs against the newly painted walls.

45. After satisfying the _____ against the property, the owners will receive $10,085 upon the close of escrow.

Leased/Least

46. We have received at _____ 30 applications for this position.

47. The _____ we can do for our displaced employees is to offer them retraining for existing jobs or four weeks' severance pay.

48. Our company uses only _____ trucks and automobiles.

49. All our _____ properties are insured through Mutual Insurance Company of America.

50. We have _____ these offices for ten years.

Lend/Loan

51. We have sufficient collateral to obtain a _____ for $1 million.

52. If the bank will not _____ us these additional funds, we will be forced to curtail our expansion.

53. Would you be able to _____ me a few minutes of your time to go over yesterday's receipts?

54. The balloon payment on this _____ is due in six months.

55. None of the financial institutions we contacted would _____ us the funds for this housing development.

Lessee/Lesser/Lessor

56. Your monthly rental checks should be made payable to TRC Management Associates, the agent for the _____.

57. You, as the _____, are responsible for any damages to the property caused by you, your family members or friends, or any other person you willingly admit to the property.

58. Because the _____ wishes to convert these apartments to condominiums, he is not renewing any leases.

59. If you elect to receive the _____ amount, the annuity payments will continue for an additional five years.

60. Are we really qualified to decide which issue is of _____ importance?

Lessen/Lesson

61. Unless we _____ our holdings in this declining area, we will continue to suffer substantial losses.

62. The federal government has _____ its controls in this area and permitted state governments to assume jurisdiction.

63. Next week's _____ will cover importing spreadsheet and database files into a word processing file.

64. Perhaps we should _____ our commitment to those areas that produce long-term results and focus temporarily on achieving some necessary short-term goals.

65. We learned our _____ when we hired someone without first checking thoroughly her references.

Levee/Levy

66. There are _____ in many places along the lower Mississippi River.

67. This tax _____ will pay for local school improvements.

68. Every government must _____ taxes to pay its expenses.

69. During the summer season many tourists use this _____ to access our resorts by boat.

70. Unpaid tax _____ against these properties have resulted in foreclosure.

Liable/Libel

71. If you do not repair the cracks in the parking lot, you will be _____ for any damages resulting from this hazardous condition.

72. The U.S. Postal Service is not _____ for any parcel unless it is insured.

73. If your evidence is not conclusive, this statement about the mayor will be construed as _____.

74. Be sure to avoid making any _____ statements in your article.

75. Our attorney believes that the company is _____ for the plaintiff's medical expenses and lost income for the past six years.

Check your answers with those given on pages 245–246 before completing the following exercise.

Reinforcement Guide 9

Instructions: Select one of the words (or a form of the word) shown below to complete each of the following sentences.

Incidence/Incidents	Its/It's	Lend/Loan
Incite/Insight	Later/Latter	Lessee/Lesser/Lessor
Indigenous/Indigent/Indignant	Lay/Lie	Lessen/Lesson
Ingenious/Ingenuous	Lean/Lien	Levee/Levy
Interstate/Intrastate	Leased/Least	Liable/Libel

1. Before occupying the premises, the _____ must sign the lease and give us a cashier's check to cover the first and last months' rent, a security deposit, and a nonrefundable cleaning fee.

2. If you need to _____ down, please use the cot in the employees' lounge.

3. Do not be deceived by his mild mannerisms and _____ smile.

4. Which financial institution has agreed to _____ us the money for this project?

5. I do not believe that our clients can be held _____ for these damages.

6. Although both her plans are sound, the accountant's _____ program for financing this project will probably be accepted by the board.

7. What kinds of plant life, besides cactus, are _____ to our local desert areas?

8. This additional .01 percent _____ on real property will remain in effect for three years only.

9. We have already _____ all the office space in this building, even before it has been completed.

10. The council canceled _____ next meeting, which was scheduled for December 23.

11. These rallies are designed to _____ college students to take a more active role in politics and elections.

12. If we _____ our advertising efforts in this area, we are certain to lose sales to our major competitor.

13. To avoid having a _____ placed against your property, you must pay these subcontractors' charges.

14. If you plan to operate _____ only, you need not comply with these federal regulations.

15. In the future please file a written report for any _____ of this nature, regardless of whether or not a customer is injured.

16. Unless you can substantiate these allegations with concrete evidence, these statements can be construed as _____.

17. For this holiday season our bank is soliciting canned goods and toys for _____ families.

18. Signed letters always _____ on her desk for a day or two before she folds and inserts them in envelopes for mailing.

19. Our _____ research staff has made another breakthrough in miniaturizing the components for our portable video cameras.

20. If you travel _____ by truck or car, you may not transport fruit, vegetables, or plants across many state lines.

Check your answers with those given on page 246 before completing the following exercise.

Name _____ Date _____

Practice Exercises for Selected Words From *Lightening/Lightning* Through *Overdo/Overdue*

Practice Guide 10

Instructions: Select the correct word or a form of the word from each set of word confusions to complete the following sentences. Write your choice in the blank provided.

Lightening/Lightning

1. What _____ agent is used in these hair-coloring products?

2. By _____ our laptop computer, we were able to gain an additional 10 percent of the market share.

3. Remind the lifeguards to prohibit swimmers from entering the pools during the summer thunder and _____ storms.

4. Several plans for _____ airport congestion are presently under consideration by the city council.

5. Metal rods are often fixed on buildings to protect them from _____.

Local/Locale

6. _____ residents are protesting the construction of this youth detention camp in their community.

7. The _____ we had originally selected for our restaurant subsequently proved to be unsuitable.

8. Can you suggest a _____ for our West Coast distribution center?

9. Which television channel in our area provides the best _____ news coverage?

10. If you are interested in learning about our _____ government, you should attend a city council meeting.

Loose/Lose

11. When did you _____ your briefcase?

12. Please call our building maintenance service to have this _____ door handle repaired.

13. If we _____ this contract, our company will suffer a substantial loss in income.

14. If these _____ tiles are not repaired immediately, someone may fall and suffer a serious injury.

15. We cannot afford to _____ the confidence of our customers.

Magnate/Magnet

16. As you navigate your boat, be sure that no _____ is nearby to distort your compass readings.

17. A Texas oil _____ has purchased these lands.

18. Although his father was a railroad _____, he was unable to achieve any kind of success with the family fortune.

19. The carnival was like a _____, attracting children and their parents from miles around.

20. Many television stars have become famous because of their _____ personalities.

Main/Mane

21. Our _____ office is located in New York City.

22. One of our _____ concerns centers around the ability of this vendor to meet our delivery schedule.

23. The trainer grabbed the lion by its _____.

24. The _____ event is scheduled to begin at 9 p.m.

25. After the race the winning jockey stroked the horse's _____.

Manner/Manor

26. I am not sure whether or not we should proceed in this _____.

27. Many nineteenth-century European _____ have been converted into hotels or tourist sights.

28. The opening scene of this movie takes place in a French _____ in the outskirts of Paris around the turn of the century.

29. Perhaps we can find a more economical _____ for packaging our products.

30. His arrogant _____ has caused us to lose several valuable employees.

Marital/Marshal/Martial

31. May we request a prospective employee to indicate his or her _____ status on an employment application?

32. Each year the dean of the college acts as _____ of the graduation exercises.

33. High school bands in the Veterans Day parade commemorated the sacrifices of veterans throughout the country with _____ music.

34. A U.S. _____ is an officer of a federal court whose duties are similar to those of a sheriff.

35. Do the current income tax laws permit a _____ deduction for a married couple filing jointly?

May be/Maybe

36. You _____ eligible for additional benefits upon retirement.

37. _____ you will be eligible for additional benefits upon retirement.

38. If you are unable to pick up this order by 5 p.m., _____ we can have it delivered to your store by a freight service.

39. As an investor in tax-free municipal bonds, you _____ interested in this new issue that has just become available.

40. This information _____ available through your local library.

Medal/Meddle

41. Do not _____ in the personal lives of your staff members.

42. How many gold _____ winners did the United States have in the last Olympics?

43. The _____ is in silver and bears on the obverse an effigy of the Queen.

44. One country should not _____ in the internal affairs of another.

45. Please do not _____ with the books or papers on my desk.

Miner/Minor

46. Because the beneficiary is still a _____, the court must appoint a conservator.

47. We cannot deal with such _____ matters at this time.

48. His father had been a coal _____ in Pennsylvania before he moved to Arizona.

49. In this state _____ may not enter into legal contracts.

50. Correct the important deficiencies in this report before you deal with the _____ errors.

Mode/Mood

51. Our supervisor always appears to be in a good _____.

52. The car is, comparatively speaking, a slow _____ of travel in the fast-paced business world.

53. What _____ will you use to pay for these purchases?

54. Natural hair styles became the _____ in the early 1980s.

55. When you are in the _____ to clean out the files, please let me know.

Moral/Morale

56. Under the direction of the new management, employee _____ has risen.

57. The team's _____ was low after its defeat.

58. Our company feels a _____ responsibility not to produce products that may be harmful to the health or well-being of society.

59. This speaker's topics all deal with _____ issues.

60. According to research, companies that sponsor profit-sharing plans have greater productivity and higher _____ than those that do not.

Morning/Mourning

61. All early _____ flights have been delayed because of the dense fog.

62. We serve complimentary coffee to our customers every _____ from 8 a.m. to 11 a.m.

63. The nation went into _____ upon the news of President Kennedy's assassination.

64. My most productive hours are those in the early _____.

65. Please do not disturb the family with business matters while they are in _____ .

Naval/Navel

66. Two students from this year's graduating class have received appointments to the _____ academy.

67. This operation will leave you with a 3-inch scar directly below the _____.

68. We purchase all our _____ oranges from distributors in Florida.

69. The senator is a graduate of Harvard and a former _____ officer.

70. Our business depends entirely upon _____ contracts.

Ordinance/Ordnance

71. A local _____ prohibits excessive noise after 10 p.m.

72. Most large cities have _____ that control the use of smog-producing fuels and other agents.

73. The army has planned to move its _____ warehouse from Seal Beach to Oceanside.

74. Which officer is in charge of _____ procurement?

75. Fines for the violation of local traffic _____ range from $25 to $200.

Overdo/Overdue

76. This invoice is already 60 days _____.

77. If you _____ the comedy scenes, you will lose your audience.

78. Two of our cooks seem to _____ the meats and vegetables.

79. His plane is already three hours _____.

80. You cannot continue to ignore your _____ bills.

Check your answers with those given on pages 247–248 before completing the following exercise.

Reinforcement Guide 10

Instructions: Select one of the words (or a form of the word) shown below to complete each of the following sentences.

Lightening/Lightning	Marital/Marshal/Martial	Morning/Mourning
Local/Locale	May be/Maybe	Naval/Navel
Loose/Lose	Medal/Meddle	Ordinance/Ordnance
Magnate/Magnet	Miner/Minor	Overdo/Overdue
Main/Mane	Mode/Mood	
Manner/Manor	Moral/Morale	

1. News of our new employee profit-sharing program has certainly boosted employee _____.

2. Because of rebel attacks on the capital, the president of the country declared a state of _____ law.

3. This _____ was selected for our next convention because of its central location.

4. The family has closed the business for three days during this _____ period.

5. We _____ interested in computerizing our billing system, so please call me for a demonstration of your software.

6. If you _____ any items while on campus, please check with the Campus Police Department.

7. The fire on the _____ base destroyed nearly $2 million in supplies and equipment.

8. Enclosed is a list of the police officers in our precinct who have received a _____ for bravery beyond the call of duty.

9. Hilton was a hotel _____ of an earlier era.

10. Because the sale and use of fireworks without a license are prohibited by a city _____, individuals may not purchase them for private Independence Day celebrations.

11. Although a seemingly _____ consideration, our all-day complimentary cookie and coffee service attracts many customers.

12. The lion's _____ had become tangled in the bars of the cage.

13. Your _____ invoices must be paid before we can ship any additional merchandise.

14. Our primary _____ of shipment is via surface carriers.

15. This _____ has been in the Winchester family for nearly two centuries.

16. _____ and thunder storms are forecast for this evening.

17. You cannot expect Johnson Industries to pay $23 million for a company and then not _____ in its internal operations.

18. Please have a _____ deliver the summons to the defendant.

19. These specialized high-quality _____ schools are designed to draw children from all parts of Los Angeles.

20. Hydro-Clor bleach may be used safely for _____ all dull, gray-looking white fabrics.

Check your answers with those given on page 248 before completing the following exercise.

WORDS OFTEN MISUSED AND CONFUSED

Practice Exercises for Selected Words From *Pair/Pare/Pear* Through *Practicable/Practical*

Practice Guide 11

Instructions: Select the correct word or a form of the word from each set of word confusions to complete the following sentences. Write your choice in the blank provided.

Pair/Pare/Pear

1. Did the chef _____ the apples before putting them in the salad?

2. The landscape design includes several Oriental _____ trees.

3. During the sale one customer purchased 17 _____ of shoes.

4. We have been directed to _____ all expenses by 10 percent during the next quarter.

5. Pictures of the bridal _____ appeared in yesterday's newspaper.

Partition/Petition

6. How many registered voters signed the _____?

7. In our new offices a _____ separates each workstation.

8. The remainder of the estate will be _____ among various relatives and friends.

9. We plan to renovate the second floor and _____ it into four medical suites.

10. Please have the client file a naturalization _____ as the first step toward obtaining United States citizenship.

Passed/Past

11. Based on this company's _____ performance, we cannot rely on it to complete a job according to schedule.

12. He has continually been _____ up for promotion.

13. In the _____ we have always closed our offices the Friday after Thanksgiving.

14. Has this information been _____ on to all our employees?

15. As a _____ award winner, you are invited to attend each annual banquet as a guest of the foundation.

Patience/Patients

16. Be sure to notify all our _____ of our new address and telephone number.

17. You will need to exhibit more _____ in dealing with clients and potential investors.

18. During this flu season the waiting room has been filled with _____ from early morning until late afternoon.

19. All new _____ must complete this information form before seeing the doctor.

20. An effective supervisor must show _____ and understanding in dealing with employees.

Peace/Piece

21. If you are interested in becoming a _____ officer, our counseling office can provide you with information about this career.

22. These offices have been leased by a new world _____ organization.

23. The _____ of land upon which ATV Industries bid contains 77 acres.

24. Most of the properties in this area are second homes owned by city dwellers who enjoy the _____ and quiet of the countryside.

25. This manufacturer's china sets all contain 144 _____.

Peal/Peel

26. At the first _____ of thunder, be sure to stop the construction crew and begin transporting the workers and equipment back to the service facility.

27. The backers knew their play was a success as _____ of laughter resounded throughout the theater.

28. Ask the chef to _____ the tomatoes before cutting them in any salads.

29. The bells _____ forth their message of Christmas joy.

30. Please inform the landlord that the paint on the outside of our office building is _____.

Peer/Pier

31. If you must _____ closely to read newspapers and magazines, you should have an optometrist check your eyes.

32. At this university, advancement in academic rank is determined solely by a committee of one's _____ .

33. Our new restaurant will be located at the end of the _____, overlooking the harbor.

34. Many of the younger children _____ at Santa Claus awhile before mustering up enough courage to approach him.

35. No night fishing is permitted on the _____.

Persecute/Prosecute

36. You must prohibit the other employees from continuing to _____ Ms. Smith.

37. During August this region is _____ by small stinging insects.

38. Has the state decided whether or not it will _____ your client?

39. Because they do not take the time to read, students _____ our clerical staff with silly questions.

40. Drunken drivers will be _____ to the fullest extent of the law.

Personal/Personnel

41. Most of our _____ have been employed by the company for over five years.

42. These benefits are for full-time _____ only.

43. Employees' _____ phone calls during working hours should be limited to emergencies only.

44. If you wish to view your _____ file, please contact the director of employee relations.

45. The former tenant still needs to remove his _____ possessions from this furnished apartment.

Perspective/Prospective

46. To increase sales, we must broaden our market _____.

47. Please have a member of our sales staff visit each of these _____ clients personally.

48. All _____ employees must submit a letter of application and a résumé.

49. To be a successful leader, one must be able to view issues in their proper _____.

50. His lack of _____ has caused us substantial losses in the foreign market.

Plaintiff/Plaintive

51. Who is the _____ in this case?

52. The _____ were unable to provide sufficient evidence to substantiate their case.

53. The _____ testimony of the witness seemingly stirred the jury.

54. The _____ has accused the defendant of fraud.

55. This particular songwriter is best known for his _____ lyrics.

Pole/Poll

56. A car has evidently crashed into and damaged this light _____.

57. A _____ of the day students has indicated that they prefer morning classes instead of afternoon classes.

58. Underground utilities free areas from unsightly telephone and electric _____.

59. For local elections there is usually a light _____.

60. In 1968 the _____ declared the election too close to call.

Populace/Populous

61. So far we have polled the _____ of three Midwestern cities.

62. Less _____ areas such as Greenview and Bellhaven have been slow in obtaining cable television.

63. Is California the most _____ state in the United States?

64. In your opinion, which of these two candidates will have greater appeal to the general _____?

65. The _____ in these regions is increasing at the rate of 4.5 percent annually.

Pore/Pour

66. Our new cleansing formula removes excess oil buildup from your _____ while keeping your skin soft and moist.

67. We will just have to _____ over this problem until we solve it.

68. The company cannot continue to _____ money into subsidiaries that fail to show reasonable earnings.

69. As the three-day weekend began, holiday travelers by the thousands _____ out of the city.

70. We spent nearly three hours _____ over past invoices to locate the cause of the discrepancy.

Practicable/Practical

71. Although your plan is _____, we do not have sufficient budget this year to finance it.

72. His three years in law school were no longer _____ when he decided to become a chemist.

73. The _____ choice would be to limit all our product warranties to six months.

74. With advancing technology and lower costs, the "robot in every broom closet" may soon become _____.

75. If the majority of consumers are indeed _____, they will not spend their time and money foolishly on this product line.

Check your answers with those given on pages 249–250 before completing the following exercise.

Reinforcement Guide 11

Instructions: Select one of the words (or a form of the word) shown below to complete each of the following sentences.

Pair/Pare/Pear
Partition/Petition
Passed/Past
Patience/Patients
Peace/Piece

Peal/Peel
Peer/Pier
Persecute/Prosecute
Personal/Personnel
Perspective/Prospective

Plaintiff/Plaintive
Pole/Poll
Populace/Populous
Pore/Pour
Practicable/Practical

1. A _____ of our employees revealed that almost 30 percent would be willing to work overtime during the inventory period.

2. If he continues to _____ the smaller children in the class, Tom will be suspended from school.

3. To function successfully as a manager, you will need to develop more _____ in dealing with difficult situations.

4. On the surface this plan appears to be the best one, but in reality it is too costly to be _____.

5. This applicant's _____ voice and mannerisms are unsuitable for the receptionist position we have open.

6. Do not allow anyone to _____ over your shoulder as you tally the daily receipts.

7. We have been audited by the Internal Revenue Service for the _____ three years.

8. If you continue to _____ over these books in such poor lighting, you will certainly damage your eyesight.

9. You must evaluate all these sudden sales increases in their proper _____.

10. The hourly _____ of our grandfather clocks often turns away potential purchasers.

11. Residents on our street signed a _____ requesting the city council to approve funds for repaving our street.

12. Franchises are available only in the less _____ cities; the other franchises have already been sold.

13. Most of our _____ are highly trained chemists or engineers.

14. Until we receive this _____ of information, the entire project remains at a standstill.

15. Please _____ at least $3,000 from this budget.

16. Our firm represents the _____ in this case.

17. We cannot afford to _____ resources into a project that has so little promise of a substantial return.

18. During the remodeling of our offices, the _____ between the two conference rooms will be removed.

19. Two _____ clients wish to discuss their investment portfolios with you.

20. The _____ of this city has remained stable since 1980.

Check your answers with those given on page 250 before completing the following exercise.

Practice Exercises for Selected Words From *Pray/Prey* Through *Scene/Seen*

Practice Guide 12

Instructions: Select the correct word or a form of the word from each set of word confusions to complete the following sentences. Write your choice in the blank provided.

Pray/Prey

1. Inexperienced investors often fall _____ to land investment schemes.

2. After each service the minister asks the congregation to _____ in silence for 30 seconds before leaving the church.

3. I _____ your forgiveness for losing these valuable papers.

4. Each year more and more people are _____ to this dreaded disease.

5. Small struggling companies are often _____ to large powerful conglomerates.

Precede/Proceed

6. The committee has decided to _____ in the usual manner with this case.

7. Please note that in each letter the reference initials should _____ the enclosure notation.

8. You may wish to _____ the demonstration with a brief overview of the capabilities of the laser printer.

9. Bill Harris _____ Jill Newcomb as president of the local chamber of commerce.

10. We will be unable to _____ with this project until early spring.

Precedence/Precedents

11. We have agreed to give _____ to all requests from the governor's office.

12. This project takes _____ over all other projects handled by our office.

13. There were no _____ for our firm's venturing into sales and production outside the United States.

14. Last year's fundraising banquet set a _____ for sponsoring this event annually.

15. In the military a general takes _____ over a captain.

Presence/Presents

16. All these _____ must be wrapped for the holiday party.

17. This subpoena requires your _____ in court on October 23.

18. Everyone in the courtroom was amazed at the calm _____ of the witness as the district attorney continued to fire questions at him.

19. Did you purchase _____ for each of the secretaries in our office?

20. The _____ of the internal auditors disrupted our office routine for nearly a week.

Principal/Principle

21. Our _____ branch in your city is located on the corner of Fifth and Main Streets.

22. How much of the _____ still remains unpaid after this year's payments?

23. If you wish to discuss this problem with the high school _____, please call her office for an appointment.

24. Not only was it a matter of _____ to bring the issue out into the open but also it was good politics.

25. Many people make it a _____ to save a regular amount from each paycheck.

Propose/Purpose

26. How do you _____ we rectify this deficit?

27. The _____ of our survey is to assess the effectiveness of our newspaper advertising.

28. After sitting and listening for over an hour, I still could not determine the _____ for the meeting.

29. Residents in the area have already begun to oppose the _____ freeway extension.

30. May I _____ that we investigate further the suitability of this site for a new branch before we make an offer on the property.

Quiet/Quite

31. These clients wish to purchase a home in a _____ residential neighborhood.

32. We were _____ disappointed when the contract was awarded to another company.

33. I am _____ sure you recognize the importance of turning in these reports on time.

34. Many executives contend that they are able to get more work done in the _____ of their homes than they are in their busy offices.

35. These charges are so serious that you should be _____ sure they are true before you proceed.

Raise/Raze/Rise

36. How much did interest rates _____ this week?

37. The city council had approved the petition to _____ this old building until a committee proved it was a historical site.

38. Last week the legislature voted to _____ the state sales tax 1/2 percent.

39. This stock _____ 16 points before it suffered any decline.

40. The old church was _____ to the ground, and a new one was built in its place.

Real/Really

41. We _____ are pleased that you will be joining our firm as a financial analyst.

42. All the consultant's suggestions have been _____ helpful in setting up our training center.

43. Working with you on this proposal has been a _____ pleasure for me.

44. Does Carnation use imitation or _____ chocolate chips in its ice cream?

45. If you are _____ concerned about the integrity of this company, perhaps you should take your business to another vendor.

Reality/Realty

46. Have you dealt with this _____ company in the past?

47. The _____ of the situation was that the company's bankruptcy left over a thousand workers unemployed.

48. After your _____ agent contacted us, we notified the buyers that you had accepted their offer.

49. From the beginning I doubted the _____ of what he had reportedly seen.

50. The company owns over $190 million worth of _____ in the Chicago downtown area.

Receipt/Recipe

51. Please consider your canceled check to be your _____.

52. Many people claim to have the _____ for See's famous fudge.

53. Is there a book that publishes _____ from famous restaurants throughout the world?

54. Save this _____ for income tax purposes.

55. Be sure to obtain a _____ for all your purchases so that you may be adequately reimbursed for your expenses.

Residence/Residents

56. _____ from the community have signed a petition to halt the airport expansion.

57. If you are interested in selling your _____, please contact me for an appraisal.

58. Please list the address of your current _____ on this form; do not list a post office box address.

59. How many _____ live in this retirement community?

60. Hotel _____ are requested to check out by 12 noon on their date of departure.

Respectably/Respectfully/Respectively

61. If your client does not address the court _____, he will be fined for contempt.

62. John, Lisa, and Karen are our senior employees; they have been with the company eight, seven, and five years, _____.

63. We insist that the nursing staff in our convalescent facility treat the patients _____.

64. Although she was a poor, struggling widow, Mrs. Smith raised her five children _____.

65. This month's first- and second-prize winners were Ann Freeman and Carl Irwin, _____.

Role/Roll

66. Congratulations upon your making the Dean's Honor _____ this semester.

67. Our senator played a major _____ in getting this piece of legislation through Congress.

68. Please have someone _____ down the sun screens each day by two o'clock to protect diners from the ocean glare.

69. Who played the _____ of Dolly in the senior class's production of *Hello, Dolly?*

70. Every instructor should have his or her _____ sheet for the opening class session.

Rote/Rout/Route

71. Most children know the alphabet by _____ before entering school.

72. The home football team _____ its opponent by a score of 40 to 7.

73. The flight _____ from Los Angeles to Indianapolis requires a stopover or a change of plane in Chicago.

74. How much _____ script learning is required of television actors and personalities?

75. What _____ should we take from the office to reach your home?

Scene/Seen

76. We have not yet _____ any results from this advertising campaign.

77. The opening _____ of the play is on Wall Street in 1929.

78. If a customer begins to create a _____, politely invite him or her into your office.

WORDS OFTEN MISUSED AND CONFUSED

79. How many times has the patient _____ Dr. Moyer?

80. I have not yet _____ the final draft of the contract.

Check your answers with those given on pages 251–252 before completing the following exercise.

Reinforcement Guide 12

Instructions: Select one of the words (or a form of the word) shown below to complete each of the following sentences.

Pray/Prey
Precede/Proceed
Precedence/Precedents
Presence/Presents
Principal/Principle
Propose/Purpose

Quiet/Quite
Raise/Raze/Rise
Real/Really
Reality/Realty
Receipt/Recipe
Residence/Residents

Respectably/Respectfully/
  Respectively
Role/Roll
Rote/Rout/Route
Scene/Seen

1. The bridesmaids—Sue Smith, Beverly Brown, and Mary Moore—require dress sizes 6, 10, and 8, _____.

2. We were _____ disappointed to learn that our company president has accepted a position with another firm.

3. Many people still follow the _____ of never doing business with friends or relatives.

4. Do not allow yourself to fall _____ to any of his investment schemes.

5. What _____ will our company play in the development and construction of the proposed new shopping center?

6. The listing _____ company has served this area for nearly twenty years.

7. When should we _____ this project to the city council?

8. We cannot _____ with this project until we obtain final approval from the federal government.

9. Most of these third-grade children already know the multiplication tables *one* through *ten* by _____.

10. You must show your _____ to exchange or return this merchandise.

11. We have received _____ a number of complaints regarding the paint quality on our bicycles.

12. Mailing this contract by 5 p.m. today takes _____ over any of our other responsibilities.

13. Unfortunately, the character part for which you have been cast appears only in the opening _____.

14. All the _____ were requested to evacuate the hotel during the emergency.

15. The builder plans to _____ the present house and construct a multimillion-dollar home in its place.

16. The only way you can ensure the _____ of this witness is to issue him a subpoena.

17. Your monthly statement shows your payment breakdown in terms of _____ and interest.

18. Our company has no written policy or _____ regarding a married couple working in the same department.

19. The police were summoned when the concert turned into a _____.

20. Whenever interest rates _____ considerably, the construction industry suffers.

Check your answers with those given on page 252 before completing the following exercise.

Practice Exercises for Selected Words From *Set/Sit* Through *Sure/Surely*

Practice Guide 13

Instructions: Select the correct word or a form of the word from each set of word confusions to complete the following sentences. Write your choice in the blank provided.

Set/Sit

1. Please _____ these boxes on the counter in my office.

2. Do not allow patients to _____ any longer than five minutes in the waiting room before recognizing their presence.

3. We _____ in the waiting room for nearly two hours before the doctor would see us.

4. Who has been _____ these dirty coffee cups on the sink instead of placing them in the dishwasher?

5. The customer has been _____ here for nearly an hour.

Sew/So/Sow

6. How often do you _____ these fields?

7. Our manager was _____ pleased with her work that he offered her a permanent position.

8. Most of the farms in this area are _____ with wheat.

9. Someone in our Alterations Department will be able to _____ the emblems on these shirts by Friday afternoon.

10. Who supplies the thread for our _____ classes?

Shall/Will

11. The corporation _____ not assume any liabilities over $1,000 not authorized specifically by the Board of Directors.

12. I _____ contact you as soon as the merchandise arrives.

13. If you are interested in viewing this property personally, we _____ be pleased to schedule an appointment.

14. Our agency _____ be responsible for screening prospective employees and furnishing information about their qualifications.

15. I _____ send you this information by the end of the week.

Shear/Sheer

16. This fabric is too _____ for the drapes in the outer office.

17. The purchase of this electric collator was a _____ waste of money.

18. The fabric has been _____ too close to the seams on all these garments.

19. From the top of the wall, there was a _____ drop of 100 feet to the sidewalk below.

20. Extreme force on the scissor handles can _____ the rivet holding the blades together.

Shone/Shown

21. The sun has not _____ for the past week in this resort area.

22. Have you _____ these plans to our new architect?

23. All these new fashions are scheduled to be _____ next month.

24. The outside lights have _____ continuously for the past week.

25. Your headlights _____ only briefly before flickering out.

Should/Would

26. If the owner is still interested in selling the property, we _____ like to make an offer.

27. I _____ have this information available within the next week.

28. When _____ I file these papers with the court?

29. If you _____ like additional information, please call my office.

30. If we _____ be able to obtain additional shipments of these silks, we will contact you immediately.

Soar/Sore

31. Prices of raw materials in our industry have continued to _____ .

32. Our new medication relieves pain from _____ and aching muscles.

33. Our hopes _____ when we heard that the contract had not yet been awarded.

34. A _____ skyscraper will replace the building on the corner of Broadway and Seventh Street.

35. You should consult a doctor about your _____ leg.

Sole/Soul

36. Our trademark is embossed on the _____ of every shoe we manufacture.

37. The _____ deterrent to our accepting this offer is the short time allowed for fulfilling the contract.

38. This artist puts her whole _____ into her work.

39. Please do not breathe a word about this merger to a _____ .

40. At present my _____ responsibility is to prepare a grant proposal for our college.

WORDS OFTEN MISUSED AND CONFUSED

Some/Somewhat

41. Although we were _____ disappointed with your last construction job, we have decided to accept your bid for the current project.

42. We will need to make _____ modifications in these plans.

43. If you wish _____ legal advice, please contact our attorney.

44. These wood carvings are _____ more expensive than we had expected.

45. A mystery novel loses _____ of its awe when read a second time.

Some time/Sometime

46. Please call our office _____ next week for an appointment.

47. Our new building should be completed _____ next month.

48. We sent you this information _____ ago.

49. If at _____ we can be of service, please let us know.

50. We have been working on this project for _____.

Staid/Stayed

51. During the holiday season most of the stores _____ open until 10 p.m.

52. Successful salespeople do not usually have _____ personalities.

53. Have you ever _____ at the Regency Hotel?

54. In the opening scene of the play, Grant portrays a _____, boring university professor.

55. If you had _____ a while longer, you would have met the new company president.

Stationary/Stationery

56. Our new _____ will be printed on beige-colored paper.

57. The _____ supplies are stored in the closet next to Ms. Dillon's desk.

58. Both the wall units are _____ fixtures in these offices.

59. Please order an additional supply of letterhead _____.

60. Interest rates have remained relatively _____ during the last month.

Statue/Stature/Statute

61. Our store specializes in clothing for men with above-average _____.

62. The architect designed a _____ to be placed in the middle of the fountain.

63. _____ in this state prohibit gambling.

64. Nearly every city has a _____ of a famous personality.

65. Bob Hope is regarded as a man of _____ by millions of Americans.

Straight/Strait

66. If you have a complaint, please take it _____ to the manager.

67. The ship caught fire at the entrance to the _____.

68. To qualify for this job, you must be able to sew a _____ seam.

69. The _____ of Gibraltar connects the Mediterranean Sea and the Atlantic Ocean.

70. The sheet feeder on our new printer does not feed in the paper _____.

Suit/Suite

71. Please reserve a _____ of rooms at the Hotel Grande for the medical convention.

72. Your _____ will be returned from our Alterations Department by Thursday afternoon.

73. Will you be able to deliver this customer's bedroom _____ by November 15?

74. This living room _____ will be placed on sale next week.

75. A _____ against your company was filed by our attorneys yesterday.

Sure/Surely

76. We are _____ pleased with the outcome of the negotiations.

77. If you need additional information, please be _____ to call me.

78. We can _____ use some additional help.

79. Our manager _____ does not understand the situation, or he would have given us additional assistance.

80. Are you _____ the door was locked when you left the office?

Check your answers with those given on pages 253–254 before completing the following exercise.

Reinforcement Guide 13

Instructions: Select one of the words (or a form of the word) shown below to complete each of the following sentences.

Set/Sit
Sew/So/Sow
Shall/Will
Shear/Sheer
Shone/Shown
Should/Would

Soar/Sore
Sole/Soul
Some/Somewhat
Some time/Sometime
Staid/Stayed
Stationary/Stationery

Statue/Stature/Statute
Straight/Strait
Suit/Suite
Sure/Surely

1. The state legislature has enacted a _____ regulating the sale of fire arms within the state.

2. I believe the owner's assessment of the value of this property is _____ exaggerated.

3. The lighthouse beacon _____ through the heavy New England fog.

4. Please _____ these figurines in the display case.

5. The Panama Canal is a _____ that connects the Atlantic and Pacific Oceans.

6. Our company plans _____ in the future to erect a branch office on this site.

7. I _____ appreciate your filling out and returning the enclosed forms as soon as possible.

8. Our factory _____ garments for well-known clothing designers on a contract basis.

9. Our offices will be relocated to a _____ on the third floor.

10. This applicant's personality is too _____ for him to be successful in the position of national sales manager.

11. Real estate prices continue to _____ as we enter a new year.

12. As soon as we receive your completed loan application, we _____ begin processing your loan.

13. You are _____ correct in assuming that this book will be available for classes next fall.

14. Please send your requests for all _____ and supplies to me.

15. There was hardly a _____ in the store at what is normally a prime shopping time.

16. In _____ desperation, the company executives decided to recall our Model 50 automatic garage door opener.

17. These _____ cabinets need to be refinished in light oak to match the remainder of the office decor.

18. We were fortunate to obtain a person of Judge Hill's _____ to deliver the graduation address.

19. My _____ concern regarding this loan centers around the applicant's ability to meet the monthly payments based upon the income shown in the application.

20. In which court will you file _____?

Check your answers with those given on page 254 before completing the following exercise.

Practice Exercises for Selected Words From *Tare/Tear/Tier* Through *Your/You're*

Practice Guide 14

Instructions: Select the correct word or a form of the word from each set of word confusions to complete the following sentences. Write your choice in the blank provided.

Tare/Tear/Tier

1. The _____ of this shipment is 1,380 pounds.

2. Only one _____ of the wedding cake was eaten.

3. You may repair this _____ in the envelope with transparent tape.

4. Please record the _____ on each bill of lading.

5. We have seats available only on the third _____ of the stadium.

Than/Then

6. You have higher seniority _____ anyone else in the department.

7. This conference is being held sooner _____ I expected.

8. You will _____ be reimbursed for your expenses.

9. As soon as escrow closes, you may _____ begin moving your possessions on to the property.

10. Certificates of deposit earn interest at a higher rate _____ money market accounts.

That/Which

11. The textbook _____ you requested is no longer in print.

12. Milton Industries, _____ is located in Albany, is our sole source for these metal bolts.

13. Your July payment, _____ we received yesterday, was $20 less than the amount stipulated in the contract.

14. One of the dining room sets _____ you shipped us arrived in damaged condition.

15. Any garments _____ are left over 30 days are subject to being sold to recover cleaning costs.

Their/There/They're

16. If _____ unable to make further payments, we must repossess the car.

17. Will you be able to meet me _____ at 2 p.m.?

18. We will provide you with samples as soon as _____ available.

19. None of _____ invoices since October have been paid.

20. Do you have _____ current address and telephone number?

Them/They

21. Was it _____ who requested this information?

22. Either we or _____ will represent the company at this conference.

23. The last two people to leave the room were _____.

24. If I were either one of _____, I would consult an attorney before taking any further action.

25. As soon as _____ arrive, I will begin the meeting.

Threw/Through

26. My secretary _____ out all these outdated files last week.

27. Only _____ your efforts and hard work were we able to obtain this contract.

28. This sale runs _____ Friday, November 21.

29. Who _____ all these papers on the floor?

30. To drive _____ the city took us nearly two hours.

To/Too/Two

31. This office is entirely _____ cold during the morning hours.

32. Please enclose the top part of your statement in the envelope _____.

33. Your clients did not seem _____ interested in purchasing the property.

34. If you wish _____ bid on the contract, please submit your formal offer by June 30.

35. _____ many of our clients have complained about the poor service in this branch office.

Us/We

36. The property was divided equally among the Johnsons, the Coxes, and _____.

37. If you were _____, would you purchase this property?

38. The managers and _____ assistants should rotate this responsibility among ourselves.

39. The manager took the visiting dignitaries and _____ on a tour of the plant.

40. The persons in charge of the project are _____, Don and I.

Vain/Van/Vane/Vein

41. Because she appears to be so _____, other employees have difficulty working with her.

42. The weather _____ on the old cottage had blown off during the storm.

43. Our new line of Ford _____ will be on display next week.

44. I tried in _____ for a week to reach him by telephone.

45. The customer complained about a large _____ of gristle in his meat.

Vary/Very

46. We were _____ pleased with the results of the survey.

47. If the writer would learn to _____ his sentence structure, his writing style would be more interesting.

48. Each month the sales in this district _____ considerably.

49. None of us are _____ interested in taking this tour.

50. Our office routine does not _____ much from day to day.

Waive/Wave

51. Be sure to _____ at the crowds along the parade route.

52. If you sign this form, you will _____ your rights to sue for malpractice.

53. Too many people think they can buy anything just by _____ money in front of other people.

54. The lawyer _____ the privilege of cross-examining the witness.

55. The announcement brought a _____ of enthusiasm.

Waiver/Waver

56. Please ask the department chair to sign this course _____.

57. If you _____ from this position, you are sure to receive criticism from your supporters.

58. Our choice _____ between Springfield and Peoria for the location of our next branch office.

59. If your client will sign this _____, we will settle this case for $15,000.

60. As the child hit the showcase, the expensive figurine _____ and then toppled and broke on the shelf.

Weather/Whether

61. Please place the daily _____ reports on my desk as soon as you receive them.

62. We have not yet decided _____ we will invest in this shopping mall.

63. Have you decided _____ to reinvest these funds or withdraw them?

64. We cannot resume work on the outside of the hotel until the _____ becomes warmer.

65. I do not believe our company will be able to _____ another financial crisis such as the last one.

Who/Whom

66. Our manager is a person _____ deals fairly with each employee.

67. I do not know to _____ this letter should be addressed.

68. _____ should I contact for an interview?

69. _____ is in charge of customer relations?

70. The only applicant _____ we have not yet interviewed is Sharon Blake.

Who's/Whose

71. Do you know _____ scheduled to work in my place tomorrow?

72. When you learn _____ briefcase was left here, please let me know.

73. Please let me know _____ rent has not yet been paid this month.

74. If you know of anyone _____ interested in renting this apartment, please let me know.

75. The person _____ last on the promotion list has little chance of being placed.

Your/You're

76. If _____ interested in applying for this position, please let us know.

77. As soon as we receive _____ verification of employment, we will approve the loan.

78. Please print _____ name legibly under the signature line.

79. Because _____ one of our best customers, we are inviting you to attend a special showing of Avant Fashions on Friday, April 3.

80. _____ certainly welcome to visit our showroom anytime to see personally the beauty and luxury of the new Sarona.

Check your answers with those given on pages 255–256 before completing the following exercise.

Reinforcement Guide 14

Instructions: Select one of the words (or a form of the word) shown below to complete each of the following sentences.

Tare/Tear/Tier
Than/Then
That/Which
Their/There/They're
Them/They
Threw/Through

To/Too/Two
Us/We
Vain/Van/Vane/Vein
Vary/Very
Waive/Wave
Waiver/Waver

Weather/Whether
Who/Whom
Who's/Whose
Your/You're

1. We do not yet know _____ we will be able to obtain the necessary financing to construct an additional wing to the hospital.

2. Most of our beauty consultants are quite _____, but clients still seek their advice and services.

3. If we were _____, we would not have entered into a contract with this particular construction firm.

4. Does the bill of lading show the _____ of the shipment?

5. Do you know _____ we can employ to reorganize our filing system?

6. Although the fire fighters' time schedules _____ from month to month, they are made available to each employee three months before taking effect.

7. We will be in these temporary offices from December 1 _____ the end of March.

8. The flight delay in Chicago held us up longer _____ we had originally expected.

9. Do you know _____ responsible for approving these budget requests?

10. If you wish, you may _____ your rights to a trial by jury.

11. Because the bank is usually _____ crowded at the noon hour, I delay making our deposits until early afternoon.

12. Our closest branch office, _____ is located at 15150 Camelback Road, would be pleased to open an account for you.

13. When _____ ready to refurnish your home, please visit our showroom.

14. The witness did not _____ once in his testimony as he was cross-examined by the defendant's attorney.

15. The manager never consults _____ employees for information or advice on customer preferences.

16. Unless you hear from me to the contrary, we will meet with the other college presidents and _____ administrative staffs on September 1.

17. The orders for those customers _____ merchandise has not yet been shipped are arranged by date in the Orders Pending file.

18. Please have the claimant sign this _____ before you disburse the settlement check.

19. The crews drilled through several _____ of hard rock before they were able to sink a well.

20. The patient is complaining that the large _____ in her legs are causing pain.

Check your answers with those given on page 256 before completing the following exercise.

WORDS OFTEN MISUSED AND CONFUSED

Additional Practice Exercises for *Affect/Effect*

Practice Guide 15, Part A

Instructions: Use a form of *affect* or *effect* to complete the following sentences.

1. What _____ do you believe this unstable stock market will have on the economy?

2. This price increase is too small to _____ our sales substantially.

3. Continued rainy weather will surely _____ adversely the completion of our new housing tract.

4. The new management has been slow in _____ any major policy changes.

5. Yesterday's announcement about our company's new PZAZZ computer had a startling _____ on the price of our stock.

6. The president's decision to reduce staff at our Burbank plant will _____ approximately 200 workers.

7. Pressure groups have been lobbying to _____ legislation that will prohibit smoking in public buildings.

8. We are yet unable to determine the _____ these new tax laws will have on our firm.

9. How can you possibly _____ additional savings when the price of raw materials continues to rise?

10. Has the laboratory been able to determine if this new medication has any side _____?

11. Unfortunately, Mr. Dunn's personal problems are beginning to _____ his job performance.

12. Overexposure to sunlight can _____ the quality of your photographs.

13. You can achieve this _____ only by following these step-by-step instructions.

14. This month *The Journal of Psychology* will feature several articles on _____ behavioral changes in emotionally disturbed children.

15. We have yet to determine the full _____ this merger will have on our employees.

Check your answers with those given on page 257 before completing the following exercise.

Practice Guide 15, Part B

Instructions: Use a form of *affect* or *effect* to complete the following sentences.

1. Do the research findings reveal that this medication will have an adverse _____ on adults over thirty?

2. Excessive rains this winter will surely _____ the completion date of our new office building.

3. What _____ will the president's speech have on stock prices?

4. The rise in the number of insurance claims in this area will _____ an increase in premium rates.

5. How were your insurance rates _____ by the recent accident?

6. Home videotape recorders have had a stimulating _____ on the revival of old movies.

7. Our new supervisor has already _____ several startling changes in the department.

8. Over 30 percent of our employees will be _____ by the impending strike.

9. How can we possibly _____ reductions in our manufacturing costs when material and labor costs continue to rise?

10. The major _____ of this new economic proposal will not be felt until the late 1990s.

11. Please determine what _____ the addition of three new microcomputers will have on our office operations.

12. None of our clients have been _____ by the recent strike in the automobile industry.

13. Long-term _____ such as these are not easily predicted.

14. Consumer furniture purchases continue to be _____ by new home construction and full employment.

15. Vigorous protests by citizens' groups may _____ legislation to prohibit the sale of identification cards by mail.

16. Have you been able to determine what _____, if any, this advertising campaign has had on sales?

17. The number of air-conditioning ducts installed with each system _____ the efficiency of the motor and the costs of operation.

18. Further investments in this company could have a substantial _____ in minimizing our losses for the current tax year.

19. Recent federal legislation will _____ several important changes in our accounting procedures.

20. Significant temperature changes in the work environment _____ the efficiency of office personnel.

Check your answers with those given on page 257 before completing the following exercise.

WORDS OFTEN MISUSED AND CONFUSED

Reinforcement Guide 15

Instructions: Use a form of *affect* or *effect* to complete the following paragraphs.

We have not yet been able to determine what _____ our new pricing policy will have on sales. With the present sales volume, we can only predict that unless our manager, Mr. Jones, can _____ significant cost reductions, this pricing policy will result in declining profits. If, on the other hand, the _____ of our present sales campaign escalates our sales volume, then we can expect the new pricing policy to be successful. In summary, sales volume and costs will _____ directly the new pricing structure initiated by Mr. Jones.

During the next quarter we will be able to analyze the overall _____ of the new policy and how it has _____ our profit picture. Before Mr. Jones is permitted to _____ any additional changes, though, the Board of Directors must review carefully how any new recommendations will _____ our entire operation in light of the potential problems that may exist with our new pricing policy. Too many unprecedented policy decisions could _____ adversely the price of our stock, and we might encounter difficulty in _____ changes to restore the price to its normal high level.

Check your answers with those given on page 257 before completing the following exercise.

Cumulative Practice Guide 1

Instructions: Select the correct alternative from the words shown in parentheses. Write your answer in the blank provided at the right of each sentence.

1. Did you know that Mr. Sooyun is (a/an) authority on rare coins? _____

2. We are not permitted to (accept/except) second-party checks. _____

3. Will you be able to (adapt/adept/adopt) this recorder to operate on 110-volt electricity? _____

4. I recommend that you follow the (advice/advise) of our tax consultant. _____

5. The strike should not (affect/effect) our sales volume immediately. _____

6. All the homes in this development have (all ready/already) been sold. _____

7. The research team was (all together/altogether) disappointed in the results of the survey. _____

8. No matter how hard he tried, Mr. Abrams was unable to (allude/elude) the persistent sales representative. _____

9. (Almost/Most) everyone in our office has contributed to the social fund. _____

10. Please divide the remaining supplies (among/between) the three offices on the second floor. _____

11. You may offer this film on a free one-week loan basis to (any one/anyone) who requests it. _____

12. May we have your check for $100, (as/like) you promised. _____

13. Can the seller (assure/ensure/insure) that the present tenants will vacate the building by May 1? _____

14. He has been treated very (bad/badly) by some of his colleagues. _____

15. Dividends are paid (biannually/biennially) on this stock—once in March and again in September. _____

16. Ex-Senator Rifkin must vacate his office in the (capital/capitol) by the first of next week. _____

17. Who will be in charge of selecting the (cite/sight/site) for our new warehouse? _____

18. The new painting in the reception area (complements/ compliments) the carpeting, draperies, and furnishings. _____

19. His (continual/continuous) complaining makes him a difficult person with whom to deal. _____

20. Only one person was absent from the (council/counsel) meeting. _____

21. All the board members were concerned about the apparent (decent/descent/dissent) among the executive officers. _____

22. The speaker continued to (deprecate/depreciate) the young candidate in the eyes of the public. _____

23. Did Ms. McKearin (device/devise) this new method for crating eggs? _____

24. Your contract is (dew/do/due) for review on the 15th. _____

25. Our South Bend factory has been known to (disburse/disperse) pollutants in the surrounding area. _____

Check your answers with those given on page 258 before completing the following exercise.

Cumulative Practice Guide 2

Instructions: Select the correct alternative from the words shown in parentheses. Write your answer in the blank provided at the right of each sentence.

1. How many responses was this ad able to (elicit/illicit)? _____

2. Do you know why the Valerios (emigrated/immigrated) from the United States? _____

3. Several of our investors feel that the collapse of savings and loan institutions is (eminent/imminent). _____

4. At least ten people have called (every day/everyday) since the ad appeared last Thursday. _____

5. Please ask (every one/everyone) to sign his or her time card each Friday. _____

6. We have asked the district attorney to investigate these charges (farther/further). _____

7. Our express lines will accommodate customers with 12 or (fewer/less) items. _____

8. Did you know that our sales manager was (formally/formerly) with the Atlas Corporation? _____

9. You did very (good/well) on the last examination. _____

10. The recent publicity has caused people to (hoard/horde) aluminum foil. _____

11. Please send copies of this report to Paul and (I/me/myself). _____

12. I did not mean to (imply/infer) that you were not doing your job properly. _____

13. Mrs. Melhorn, our company president, reminds us frequently of her (indigenous/indigent/indignant) beginnings. _____

14. Once we expand our operations to Virginia and Delaware, we will be subject to all laws governing (interstate/intrastate) commerce. _____

15. The company must expand (its/it's) sales force by January 1. _____

16. Please ask Ms. Feldman to (lay/lie) down. _____

17. Unfortunately, Ron is (liable/libel) for the debts incurred by his partner. _____

18. The belt on this wheelchair motor appears to be too (loose/lose). _____

19. Many of our customers find Mr. Brown's (marital/marshal/ martial) manner offensive. _____

20. (May be/Maybe) one of our consultants can help you solve this problem. _____

21. There has definitely been a decline in employee (moral/morale) since the new executive group took over the operations. _____

22. Caution our readers not to (overdo/overdue) this exercise program. _____

23. Three years have (passed/past) since I was transferred to the East Coast. _____

24. I admire your (patience/patients) in dealing with all these production problems. _____

25. This is not the first time the manager has been charged with (persecuting/prosecuting) one of his employees. _____

Check your answers with those given on page 258 before completing the following exercise.

Cumulative Practice Guide 3

Instructions: Select the correct alternative from the words shown in parentheses. Write your answer in the blank provided at the right of each sentence.

1. On this application you are not required to disclose any (personal/personnel) information. _____

2. Be sure to send copies of this brochure to all (perspective/ prospective) clients. _____

3. You must obtain Ms. Goto's approval before you (proceed/ precede) any further with this research. _____

4. All accounts marked with a star must be given (precedence/precedents). _____

5. If I felt he were a person of (principal/principle), I would gladly enter into this agreement. _____

6. This office needs peace and (quiet/quite) for a few days. _____

7. Do you expect the price of gold to (raise/rise) within the next few weeks? _____

8. Our personnel manager is (real/really) impressed with the qualifications of these applicants. _____

9. Contact at least three (reality/realty) firms for an appraisal of this property. _____

10. Did you obtain a (receipt/recipe) for your October payment? _____

11. Mr. Webb (respectfully/respectively) requested the governor to review his petition. _____

12. What (wrote/rote/route/rout) will the truck take from El Paso to Chicago? _____

13. Please (set/sit) the heavy packages on the counter. _____

14. Whom have you employed to (sew/so/sow) the costumes for our grand opening? _____

15. I have never before seen a customer with such (shear/sheer) gall. _____

16. If we could have your order (some time/sometime) before November 1, we can guarantee delivery before Christmas. _____

17. None of the walls on this floor are (stationary/stationery). _____

18. The (statue/stature/statute) of this art object is too great for the museum patio. _____

19. Your travel agent is (sure/surely) pleased with the arrangements he was able to make for you. _____

20. At present we have more orders for this electronic game (than/then) we have inventory in our warehouse. _____

21. Before we can make any recommendations, we must study (their/there/they're) operations more fully. _____

22. Dr. Mendoza takes (to/too/two) personally the problems of her patients. _____

23. Many of us believe the zoning commission will (waiver/waver) once it is confronted with the citizens' demands. _____

24. All employees have been instructed not to disclose (weather/whether) our stock will go public. _____

25. (Your/You're) one of the leading contenders for this position. _____

Check your answers with those given on page 258 before completing the following exercise.

Name _____ Date _____

Cumulative Practice Guide 4

Instructions: Select the correct words from the word con [Pg 185 -186 187 -188] s in the following letter. Write your answers in the numbered bla

Dear Mr. Newsome:

(Your, You're) request to refinance your plumbing and

hardware supply has been tentatively approved. When we

receive your (explicit, implicit) written statement that you will   2. _____

(accede, exceed) to our request to place as additional collateral   3. _____

your newly acquired plant (cite, sight, site), we will be able to   4. _____

initiate the formal paperwork.

Please excuse our delay in answering your request; we were

under the (allusion, delusion, illusion) that you were also seeking   5. _____

financing elsewhere to (ensure, insure) sufficient (capital, capitol) 6. _____

for your expansion program. As you know, we are (principal,   7. _____

principle) lenders only and do not provide secondary financing.   8. _____

The opinions of (every one, everyone) on our loan committee   9. _____

were (all together, altogether) favorable, and the members   10. _____

agreed to approve the loan tentatively. (Their, There, They're)   11. _____

only concern was that the amount requested is in (access,   12. _____

excess) of the present (appraised, apprised) value of your   13. _____

business. Consequently, we are requesting the additional

collateral before we (precede, proceed) with this loan any   14. _____

(farther, further).   15. _____

Speaking for the entire loan committee, I can (assure,   16. _____

ensure, insure) you that we will (dew, do, due) everything   17. _____

possible to assist you with your financing needs. We (to,   18. _____

too, two) are interested in the growth and development of

this community and wish to encourage (perspective,   19. _____

prospective) investors.

Please contact me as soon as possible to arrange a
meeting to tie up the (loose, lose) ends. We should not (defer,
differ) getting the paperwork under way any longer. Any
afternoon next week will be (all right, alright) with me; the
sooner we have this meeting, the sooner we will be able to
(disburse, disperse) your funds.

I look forward to hearing from you and appreciate that
you (choose, chose) our bank to obtain your (capital, capitol)
funding.

Sincerely yours,

20. _____

21. _____

22. _____

23. _____

24. _____

25. _____

The answers to this exercise appear in the **Instructor's Manual and Key for HOW 7: A Handbook
for Office Workers, Seventh Edition.**

WORDS OFTEN MISUSED AND CONFUSED

Cumulative Practice Guide 5

Instructions: Select the correct words from the word confusions shown in parentheses in the following memorandum. Write your answers in the numbered blanks that appear at the right.

TO: Karen Williams, Director of (Personal, Personnel)   1. _____

FROM: Gary Morgan, Executive Vice President

SUBJECT: THE (AFFECT, EFFECT) OF RECRUITMENT,   2. _____
          SELECTION, AND IN-SERVICE TRAINING ON
          OVERALL PLANT OPERATIONS

    I wish to (complement, compliment) you on the excellent job   3. _____

you did in recruiting and hiring (personal, personnel) for our new   4. _____

plant that opened last year. You are to be (commanded,   5. _____

commended) for adding such a large number of new employees

during such a short time period.

    Our production and sales this year will (accede, exceed) last   6. _____

year's by 30 percent. Much of this increase is (dew, due, do) to   7. _____

your (continual, continuous) efforts to hire and train well-   8. _____

qualified people.

    Last year when we set a (precedence, precedent) in the   9. _____

industry by staffing an entire plant with predominantly new

employees, I was concerned (weather, whether) or not this   10. _____

action would adversely (affect, effect) our production. However,   11. _____

my concern was (shear, sheer) nonsense. The people you have   12. _____

hired are more qualified, efficient, and dependable (than, then)   13. _____

I had expected. I wish to (formally, formerly) congratulate you   14. _____

on your progressive personnel practices.

    May I also indicate that I agree in (principal, principle) with 15. _____

the extensive in-service training program you have initiated. We

have (all ready, already) promoted a number of people from   16. _____

within the company, and this policy of internal promotion has

certainly helped the (moral, morale) of all (who, whom) work   17. _____

here. Although the cost of this in-service program is (expansive,   18. _____

expensive), it appears to be worth the investment. Other

19. _____

members of the executive staff (appraise, apprise) this

20. _____

program in the same manner.

    Your contributions and innovative ideas have (allowed,

21. _____

aloud) us to plan for the future with a (confidant, confident)

22. _____

outlook. We will keep you informed of our (coarse, course)

23. _____

of action so that we may continue to rely on your (assistance,

24. _____

assistants) to (assure, ensure, insure) our continued success.

25. _____

*The answers to this exercise appear in the **Instructor's Manual and Key for HOW 7: A Handbook for Office Workers, Seventh Edition.***

                                                               WORDS OFTEN MISUSED AND CONFUSED

Testing Your Understanding, Part 1 (2 points each)

Instructions: Read the following sentences carefully for meaning. If a word has been used incorrectly, UNDERLINE it. Then write the correct word in the blank at the right of the sentence. If a sentence is correct, write *OK* in the blank.

1. At the present time I am adverse to accepting any additional
   responsibilities. _____

2. Our clients' annual income exceeds the minimum requirement
   for this home by $8,450. _____

3. Upon the advise of our attorney, we have decided not to invest
   in this property. _____

4. Large increases in materials costs have affected price
   increases in nearly all our products. _____

5. A large amount of stockholders have protested our proposal to
   merge with ICA Corporation. _____

6. Although we cannot ensure that these condominiums will be
   ready for occupancy on October 1, we are promising
   purchasers this date. _____

7. Our company has born financial burdens since the early 1990s. _____

8. The state game licensing bureau is located in Room 480 of the
   California State Capital. _____

9. This manual explains how to sight sources and prepare
   footnotes for term papers and reports. _____

10. To receive your complementary copy, just fill out and return
    the enclosed postcard. _____

11. A number of credible financial institutions are endorsing the
    new issue of our stock. _____

12. You may wish to seek counsel from your attorney before
    making a decision on this issue. _____

13. Companies that continue to disburse pollutants in the
    environment will be fined heavily. _____

14. Not everyone is familiar with the works of the imminent
    English playwright Shakespeare. _____

15. Most of the employees in our organization have immigrated
    from Mexico. _____

16. Almost everyday we receive a complaint about the service in
    our Denver office. _____

17. What effect has this advertising campaign had on sales? _____

18. The police in this area are attempting to stop the elicit sale of drugs.

_____

19. Every one in the company should receive this information on employee medical and retirement benefits.

_____

20. Do you foresee any substantial decent in interest rates within the next three months?

_____

21. At yesterday's meeting the board disproved the purchase of these desert properties.

_____

22. Although many people depreciate the commercialism associated with Christmas, they still join the millions of holiday shoppers.

_____

23. Personalized sales letters tend to elicit a greater response than nonpersonalized ones.

_____

24. The stories being sent by these foreign correspondents seem hardly creditable.

_____

25. Our new file clerk is continuously misplacing or misfiling important documents.

_____

26. Buckingham Palace is a frequently visited tourist site in London.

_____

27. These two textbooks compliment each other; what one touches upon lightly, the other delves into heavily.

_____

28. His employer censored him for neglecting his work.

_____

29. All these Italian chains are 18-carat gold.

_____

30. How many people have you hired to canvas neighborhoods in the vicinities of our three offices?

_____

31. You may obtain this information from any one of my assistants.

_____

32. If you wish to invest any additional capitol in this project, please let me know.

_____

33. Who beside you in the office has been able to get tickets to the opening game of the World Series?

_____

34. I feel badly that we are unable to offer you a position at the present time.

_____

35. I have learned to pack only the bare necessities for my business trips.

_____

36. Anytime you are interested in learning more about real estate investments, just give me a call at 555-7439.

_____

37. Have you appraised anyone on the staff of the change in your plans?

_____

38. Like I stated in my July 16 memo, we will continue to honor the 25 percent discount on all our products in the FS-200 series line through July 31.

_____

39. The rapid assent of interest rates during the last three weeks has curtailed the home-buying market considerably. _____

40. Between all of us, we should be able to devise a plan to solve this problem. _____

41. Most everyone on our staff has attended at least one of your computer seminars. _____

42. We have not all together determined the projected final cost of this construction project. _____

43. The cause of cancer continues to allude all medical researchers. _____

44. Effective television advertising creates an allusion of reality in the minds of viewers. _____

45. Fluctuations in oil prices effect consumer automobile purchasing patterns. _____

46. Unless you adopt readily to change, you will have difficulty working for such a progressive, forward-looking company like CompuServe. _____

47. We are unable to except these expired coupons. _____

48. You will need a court order to obtain excess to the files. _____

49. You may wish to seek advice from your accountant before selling these properties. _____

50. What kind of affect, if any, will the retail clerks' strike have on our industry? _____

*The answers to this exercise appear in the **Instructor's Manual and Key for HOW 7: A Handbook for Office Workers, Seventh Edition**.*

Testing Your Understanding, Part 2 (2 points each)

Instructions: Read the following sentences carefully for meaning. If a word has been used incorrectly, UNDERLINE it. Then write the correct word in the blank at the right of the sentence. If a sentence is correct, write *OK* in the blank.

1. Unless you give implicit instructions to our administrative assistant, the job will not be done correctly.   _____

2. Most of our extant projects have been financed by Washington Federal Bank.   _____

3. Less people than we had expected responded to our newspaper advertisements.   _____

4. If you were me, would you accept this position?   _____

5. Trees from which we obtain this kind of lumber are indigent of the Northwest.   _____

6. These books have lain on the shelves for years without anyone's even opening them.   _____

7. We are not libel for any damage caused by the trucking company.   _____

8. If you are interested in purchasing additional computers, we maybe able to obtain them for you at discount prices.   _____

9. A local ordnance prohibits gambling within the city limits.   _____

10. If the manager continues to prosecute members in his department, they will file a formal grievance against him.   _____

11. How many hours did our assistants pore over books in the law library before finding these legal precedents?   _____

12. Our principle stockholder has expressed opposition to our acquiring additional properties in this area.   _____

13. Before constructing any type of building on this property, we will need to raise the existing structures.   _____

14. The founder of our company played a major roll in the development of our city.   _____

15. We may sometime in the future be able to do business with you.   _____

16. When did the state legislature enact this stature?   _____

17. As a result of there inquiry, the grand jury has begun an investigation.   _____

18. Only the department chair can waive this requirement.   _____

19. Within the last decade persons involved in realty sales have been forced to whether periods of high interest rates. _____

20. Since you are located further from the airport than I, I will pick up the shipment. _____

21. As long as you continue to flaunt authority and proper work ethics, you will have difficulty holding a job. _____

22. You did good on this examination. _____

23. A hoard of reporters surrounded the rock star as he stepped from his limousine. _____

24. Did the vice president infer that our manager had been replaced because our office has shown a declining sales record? _____

25. During the last two years, the company has reached it's sales quotas six of the eight quarters. _____

26. If the bank will loan us the money, we will be able to enlarge our restaurant. _____

27. Please have the marshal subpoena this witness. _____

28. We would appreciate your sending us a check to settle your overdo account. _____

29. Please refer any perspective clients to me personally. _____

30. A pole of our employees revealed that the majority preferred receiving stock options and benefit programs over salary increases. _____

31. Which of these requests should receive precedence? _____

32. We are real enthusiastic about the possibility of Thornton Industries acquiring our company. _____

33. Rote learning does not come easily to most people. _____

34. Hurricane-like winds sheered the roofs off three houses in this Florida neighborhood. _____

35. Our new stationary has been ordered and should arrive within the next week. _____

36. At the present time we have more employees in this branch office then we need. _____

37. There are to many students enrolled in this class. _____

38. No matter how intimidating the opposition may be, do not waiver if you feel your position is correct. _____

39. We called a consultant who we had met in Atlanta. _____

40. If your interested in these kinds of investment opportunities, please give me a call. _____

41. Only if someone in your family is willing to sign a guaranty can we approve this loan.
_____

42. Because this sales territory includes California, Oregon, Washington, Nevada, and Arizona, my job involves considerable intrastate travel.
_____

43. Our goal is to establish branch offices in the most populace areas of the state.
_____

44. Most of the residence in this convalescent home are in need of constant care and supervision.
_____

45. Since all our floor models will be placed on sale this weekend, you may wish to select a bedroom suit at that time.
_____

46. If home prices continue to sore, fewer and fewer people will be able to purchase single-family dwellings in our city.
_____

47. Our personnel manager could not overlook such a fragrant violation of company policy.
_____

48. Students from almost every cultural hew attend our university.
_____

49. Such an ingenious plan should surely give us a competitive advantage in marketing our new video cameras.
_____

50. Please have someone from our maintenance crew repair this lose door plate before one of our students trips and falls.
_____

*The answers to this exercise appear in the **Instructor's Manual and Key for HOW 7: A Handbook for Office Workers, Seventh Edition.***

Section 8   Grammar and Usage

Noun Plurals (8-4)

Practice Guide 1

Instructions: Write the plural form for each item given below. Use the blank provided at the right of each item.

1. policy _____
2. church _____
3. radio _____
4. life _____
5. Montgomery _____
6. tomato _____
7. curriculum _____
8. statistics _____
9. mumps _____
10. brigadier general _____
11. yes and no _____
12. cupful _____
13. bookshelf _____
14. brother-in-law _____
15. basis _____
16. pants _____
17. 9 _____
18. roof _____
19. attorney _____
20. waltz _____
21. alto _____
22. cargo _____
23. this and that _____
24. monkey _____
25. analysis _____

26. alumnus _____
27. per diem _____
28. county _____
29. box _____
30. Koltz _____
31. A _____
32. bronchus _____
33. lessee _____
34. father figure _____
35. father-in-law _____
36. valley _____
37. R.N. _____
38. Ms. Ross _____
39. datum _____
40. Mickey Mouse _____
41. going-over _____
42. t _____
43. jockey _____
44. Japanese _____
45. Mr. Ramirez _____
46. embargo _____
47. yourself _____
48. chassis _____
49. half _____
50. German _____

Check your answers with those given on page 259 before completing the following exercise.

Practice Guide 2

Instructions: From the context of the following letter, first underline all those nouns that should be written in plural form. Then write the correct spellings in the blank lines given below.

Dear Mr. Washington:

According to our staff of analyst, there are several basis on which your tax were determined. Separate analysis from three of our staff member are enclosed.

As your attorney, we advise you to appeal individually the assessed valuation of two property; the other seven property appear to have been assessed correctly. If we can assist you with the proceeding, please call one of our secretary to set up an appointment within the next two week.

In order to protest the two assessment, we will have to collect sufficient datum to show the value of other duplex in the area. Both Mr. Avery would be able to help us gather this information. One of the major criterion will be the average price of comparable real estate turnover during the last six month. Another factor will be the assessed valuation of other such property in both the Borden and Simi Valley. Survey of three or four real estate agency should provide the appropriate information to assist us with these two case.

We believe there is an excellent opportunity to have the tax assessment on both these duplex reduced considerably. Please let us know if we may be of assistance to you.

Sincerely yours,

1. _____   10. _____   19. _____

2. _____   11. _____   20. _____

3. _____   12. _____   21. _____

4. _____   13. _____   22. _____

5. _____   14. _____   23. _____

6. _____   15. _____   24. _____

7. _____   16. _____   25. _____

8. _____   17. _____

9. _____   18. _____

*The answers to this exercise appear in the **Instructor's Manual and Key for HOW 7: A Handbook for Office Workers, Seventh Edition.***

Noun Possessives (8-5)

Practice Guide 3

Instructions: So that each of the following sentences will read correctly, write in the blank at the right the proper form of the word(s) shown in parentheses.

1. Our (son-in-law) business went bankrupt last month. _____

2. The (child) bicycles were stolen from the garage. _____

3. (Everyone else) room was locked. _____

4. Yesterday Ms. Purdy gave the boss a (week) notice. _____

5. Three members of the (personnel manager) association agreed to speak to our class. _____

6. The (Ross) and (Lopez) mountain cabin was damaged severely during the snowstorm. _____

7. The (girl) softball team will participate in the championship playoffs. _____

8. A file of delinquent accounts is kept in (Mr. Beaty) office. _____

9. (Bob) and (Phil) offices are located in Suite 454. _____

10. This (company) stock declined sharply during the last six months. _____

11. The store manager moved (lady) apparel from the second floor to the third floor. _____

12. You are still responsible for four (month) interest on this loan. _____

13. (Mary) receiving the scholarship was no surprise to me. _____

14. (Mrs. Jones) car was parked illegally. _____

15. The (chief of police) answer did not satisfy the reporters. _____

16. (Alumnus) children receive preferential consideration for admission to our college. _____

17. (ITT) investment in new equipment this year amounted to $18 million. _____

18. The (lease) expiration date is July 30. _____

19. Do you carry (man) and (boy) clothing? _____

20. (Martha) and (Don) house was sold yesterday. _____

Check your answers with those given on page 259 before completing the following exercise.

Practice Guide 4

Instructions: From the context of the following letter, first underline all those nouns that should be written in the possessive form. Then write the correct spelling in one of the blank lines given below.

Dear Ms. Huffman:

Because of your companys outstanding payment record, we are extending an invitation to you to increase your credit limit. This months charges on your account reached $5,600, $600 beyond your present limit. If you wish to extend your credit line to $7,500, all we need is your Purchasing Departments approval and Mrs. Kellys signature on the enclosed application.

Next month we will be distributing our holiday sales catalog. This seasons merchandise is even more exciting than last seasons. You will see by your salespeoples enthusiasm that we have the best product line in our history. Childrens toys are more advanced than ever before with electronic game toys promising to be best-sellers. Also, for this year the number of items in boys and girls wearing apparel has nearly doubled.

By distributing our catalog early in August, we hope to get a two months head start on the season. With everyones cooperation we can have record-breaking sales this year. Our managers new shipping program can have any of the catalog merchandise at your door with only seven working days notice.

To encourage buyers early orders, we are offering a 25 percent discount on all babys clothing and furniture ordered during September. Similar discounts are being offered on mens clothing and ladys lingerie. Take advantage of Septembers savings; place your order when the holiday catalog arrives. Turn todays savings into future profits.

Sincerely,

1. _____	8. _____	15. _____
2. _____	9. _____	16. _____
3. _____	10. _____	17. _____
4. _____	11. _____	18. _____
5. _____	12. _____	19. _____
6. _____	13. _____	20. _____
7. _____	14. _____	

The answers to this exercise appear in the **Instructor's Manual and Key for HOW 7: A Handbook for Office Workers, Seventh Edition.**

Pronouns (8-6 through 8-8)

Practice Guide 5

Part 1. Subjective- and objective-case pronouns. From the choices given in parentheses, select the correct pronoun form. Write your answer in the blank line given at the right of each sentence.

1. (We, Us) secretaries are planning a surprise party for Ms. Phillips. _____

2. Be sure to give a copy of the sales receipt to Ron or (I, me, myself). _____

3. Speaking of Mr. Reynolds, that was (he, him) on the telephone. _____

4. Mr. Ryan is more likely to receive the appointment than (I, me). _____

5. I would not want to be (she, her) when our sales manager discovers the error. _____

6. Dr. Boyer asked (we, us) nurses to work overtime during the epidemic. _____

7. The person at the end of the hall could not have been (he, him). _____

8. The receptionist mistook my brother to be (I, me). _____

9. I would prefer to send the letter to Ms. Cook rather than (she, her). _____

10. We, John and (I, me), plan to attend the convention. _____

Check your answers with those given on page 259 before completing the following exercise.

Part 2. Subjective- and objective-case pronouns. If a pronoun is used correctly in the following sentences, write *OK* in the blank line. If a pronoun is used incorrectly, underline the error and write the correction in the blank line.

1. Between you and I, I believe this new microchip will revolutionize the industry. _____

2. Did you say that the top salesperson was her? _____

3. I was taken to be her at the company Halloween party. _____

4. The person who ordered the new equipment must have been him. _____

5. Copies of the announcement were sent to us, Paul and myself. _____

6. Dr. Rich asked Teri and I to cancel his appointments for the remainder of the day. _____

7. Ms. Allison knows as much about this contract as I.

        _____

8. Three accountants—Bob, Arlene, and me—attended the convention in Chicago.

        _____

9. If you were me, what decision would you have made?

        _____

10. I would not want to be he under these circumstances.

        _____

Check your answers with those given on page 260 before completing the following exercise.

Part 3. *Who* and *whom* pronouns. From the choices given in parentheses, select the correct form. Write your answer in the blank line given at the right of each sentence.

1. Our company needs an engineer (who, whom) understands construction design.

        _____

2. Do you know (who, whom) Mr. Reece selected to serve as his assistant?

        _____

3. We do not know (who, whom) the real estate agent could have been.

        _____

4. John is a person (who, whom) I believe will perform well under pressure.

        _____

5. (Whoever, Whomever) acts as chairman of the committee will have an advantage.

        _____

6. Elizabeth Jones is the person (who, whom) we believe will be elected.

        _____

7. (Who, Whom) did John recommend for the position?

        _____

8. Ms. Hill is courteous to (whoever, whomever) enters the office.

        _____

9. Please list the names of the staff members (who, whom) you think will participate in the contest.

        _____

10. My supervisor, (who, whom) you met yesterday, will retire next year.

        _____

11. (Whoever, Whomever) arrives at the airport first should check on our reservations.

        _____

12. Call me as soon as you learn (who, whom) has been awarded the contract.

        _____

13. Mr. Dorman may have been the agent (who, whom) we contracted originally.

        _____

14. I cannot imagine (who, whom) you thought him to be.

        _____

15. I do not know (who, whom) the newest member of the board could be.

        _____

Check your answers with those given on page 260 before completing the following exercise.

GRAMMAR AND USAGE

Practice Guide 6

Instructions: From the context of the following letter, first underline all those pronouns that are used incorrectly. Then write the correct pronouns in the blank lines given below.

To the Staff:

During the next month us nurses must renew our parking permits. Be sure to bring the old permit to either Mr. Feinberg or myself before April 30. Mr. Feinberg is in the office longer hours than me, so perhaps you may find leaving your present parking permit with him more convenient than leaving it with me. The person issuing the new parking permits will be him.

All of us—you, the other nurses, and I—will be prohibited from parking in the visitors' parking lot. The hospital security staff has been instructed to issue tickets to whoever they find illegally parked. This restriction will be implemented because our chief administrator, Ms. Takagi, has received numerous complaints about the crowded condition of this lot. It was her who decided that this lot would be closed to all staff members, no matter whom the individual may be or what his or her position may entail. I realize that a number of the staff may be annoyed with Ms. Takagi's decision. Under these circumstances I would not want to be her. Between you and I, though, I believe that our chief administrator had no other alternative.

Ms. Takagi has asked we employees to park in Lot C, which is located in our high-rise parking facility. An additional security guard, who Mr. Feinberg recently employed, will patrol this employee parking area during the evening hours. The new security officer, Ian Davis, has asked Mr. Feinberg and I to inform you of his presence. He will be pleased to help whomever needs his assistance with any parking problems. Ian is a person whom I believe will be an excellent addition to our hospital staff.

If you have any questions about the new parking regulations, please be sure to consult me personally.

1. _____   6. _____   11. _____

2. _____   7. _____   12. _____

3. _____   8. _____   13. _____

4. _____   9. _____   14. _____

5. _____   10. _____   15. _____

*The answers to this exercise appear in the **Instructor's Manual and Key for HOW 7: A Handbook for Office Workers, Seventh Edition.***

Verbs (8-10 through 8-18)

Practice Guide 7

Instructions: If the verb is used correctly in the following sentences, write OK in the blank line following the sentence. If the verb is used incorrectly, underline the error and write the correct form in the blank line.

1. Have you wrote letters to the two agencies?   _____

2. The tract of new homes were laid out attractively.   _____

3. Our client has already spoke to several agents in your firm.   _____

4. The patient asked if he could lay down on the cot.   _____

5. Has the criteria been ranked in the order of their importance?   _____

6. There is several alternatives you may wish to consider.   _____

7. Neither of us wish to postpone his vacation.   _____

8. One fourth of the light bulbs in this shipment were broken.   _____

9. Dr. Sanders is one of those doctors who knows a great deal about law.   _____

10. Our stock of felt-tip pens have disappeared from the supply cabinet.   _____

11. He had forgot about this appointment until his secretary reminded him.   _____

12. Until last Wednesday the book had laid on top of the counter.   _____

13. All the juice in these bottles have been drunk.   _____

14. Between the two bookcases was a locked cabinet.   _____

15. Neither you nor the other accountant have been absent this year.   _____

16. Each sofa, chair, and table needs to be replaced.   _____

17. The staff was arguing loudly about their duties.   _____

18. One of the mothers have consented to bring donuts for the class.   _____

19. All our bills for this month have been payed.   _____

20. Either Allen or Nanette is to receive the commission for this sale.   _____

Check your answers with those given on page 260 before completing the following exercise.

Practice Guide 8

Instructions: As you read the following paragraphs, first underline all the verb forms that are used incorrectly. Then write the correct answers in the blanks provided below.

To: Mr. Pflum

In national medical journals we have ran several ads describing our new disposable thermometers. Although the number of responses we have received to these ads have been great, the staff is in disagreement as to whether this advertising mode should be continued. One of the officers feel strongly that we have exhausted the market reached by the medical journals. She believes local distribution channels or direct mail advertising are more effective than national advertising.

Hospitals is the main users of our disposable thermometers. Our supply of these thermometers are almost depleted because one of the clerks in our main office had forgot to notify the factory to manufacture an additional supply. We have spoke to him about this matter, and he has took steps to prevent this error from occurring again. In the clerk's defense, however, we must consider that a large number of these disposable thermometers had laid in our warehouse for over four months without our filling any orders from this supply. All the orders was filled directly from the factory.

Dr. Maedke is one of those doctors who has supported the use of disposable thermometers since their introduction. He believes that every doctor's office, medical clinic, and hospital need to use this kind of thermometer; it is more sanitary and economical than the conventional thermometer. Dr. Maedke has brung out this concept in a number of the speeches he has given at national medical conventions. We are fortunate to have the support of a person who are so well-known in the profession.

We are looking forward to this product becoming a top seller. Although advertising in medical journals has payed for itself, two members of the staff prefers alternate methods of advertising. Neither of them, though, have yet offered specific advertising plans. When the media for future advertising has been selected, we will let you know.

1. _____   8. _____   15. _____

2. _____   9. _____   16. _____

3. _____   10. _____   17. _____

4. _____   11. _____   18. _____

5. _____   12. _____   19. _____

6. _____   13. _____   20. _____

7. _____   14. _____

The answers to this exercise appear in the **Instructor's Manual and Key for HOW 7: A Handbook for Office Workers, Seventh Edition.**

Part 3

Key to Familiarization Exercise for HOW (pages 3–11)

Answer	Section		Answer	Section
1. c	Preface, page vi		26. a	1-1
2. d	Preface, page vi		27. d	4-9
3. b	Preface, page vi		28. d	11-7
4. b	Preface, page vi, and inside front cover		29. b, c	2-5g, h; 2-6d
			30. b, d	3-5a, c, d
5. c	Preface, page vi		31. b	page 171
6. c	10-10		32. b, c	3-4
7. b	15-12, 15-18h		33. d	1-5a
8. c	14-1, 14-2, 14-3		34. b, c	2-2a, b, f, h
9. a	Preface, page vi		35. b, d	11-10
10. d	page 141		36. a, d, e, f, g	2-5a, e; 2-6a, c
11. b	1-33, 1-41e		37. b	11-24b
12. c, d	3-8e		38. a	4-4, 4-5b, 4-6, 4-7
13. b	4-2a, b, c		39. d	10-10
14. b, c, d	2-4a		40. a, d, e	11-8b, c
15. a, c, d	8-7b		41. a, e	8-12
16. b, d	8-21		42. a, d	3-7a
17. a, c, d	3-9a, c		43. d	11-20, 11-33
18. d, e	6-1a		44. c	4-4a, b, c
19. c	1-15a, d		45. a, c, d	page 141
20. b	1-2		46. b, d	6-1a
21. a, b	11-11b		47. a, d	4-1a, b, c, d
22. b, c	8-4b		48. d	1-19
23. c, d	page 144		49. b, d	1-55a, c, d, e
24. b	3-1d		50. b, c	page 166
25. c, d	8-18f			

Key to Practice Exercises

Section 1   Punctuation

Practice Sentences 1 (page 17)

1. . . . rain, sleet, and ice . . . .
2. . . . uses a word processor, prepares spreadsheets, and answers . . . .
3. . . . Arizona, Nevada, Utah, and Montana.
4. . . . changed all the locks, barred the outside windows, and installed . . . .
5. Trees, shrubs, and ground cover . . . .
6. Call Henry Smith, offer him the job, and ask . . . .
7. Many doctors, dentists, and lawyers . . . .
8. . . . obtained a permit, purchased the building materials, and hired . . . .
9. Proofread the report, make three copies, and mail . . . .
10. . . . stationery store, post office, and grocery store . . . .

Practice Paragraph 1 (page 17)

1. . . . inventory, sales, and profit picture.
2. . . . high inventory, low sales volume, and declining profits . . . .
3. Write the letter, sign it, and mail it.

Practice Sentences 2 (page 19)

1. In fact, ...
2. . . . , nevertheless, ...
3. . . . , fortunately, ...
4. Yes, ...
5. . . . , in other words, ...
6. Between you and me, ...
7. No commas preferred. (Optional commas around *therefore*).
8. . . . , without a doubt.
9. No commas. (*Perhaps* flows smoothly into the rest of the sentence.)
10. No commas preferred. (Optional commas around *indeed*.)

Practice Paragraph 2 (page 19)

1. We, as a rule, ...
2. However, ...
3. Perhaps you will . . . . (No commas.)
4. I can, of course, ...

Practice Sentences 3 (page 21)

1. Brett, ...
2. . . . , class, ...
3. . . . , Mrs. Davis.
4. . . . , ladies and gentlemen, ...
5. . . . , Gary, ...
6. Yes, fellow citizens of Spokane, ...

7. No commas.
8. ..., Dr. Bush.
9. No commas.
10. ..., friends and neighbors, ...

Practice Paragraph 3 (page 21)

1. ..., Ms. White, ...
2. ..., Ms. Smith.
3. Gentlemen, ...

Practice Sentences 4 (page 23)

1. ..., Stan Hughes, ...
2. ..., the author of a best-seller, ...
3. ..., a member of the finance committee, ...
4. No commas.
5. ..., "Skiing in California," ...?
6. No commas.
7. ..., our new assistant, ...
8. ..., two prominent authorities on the subject of consumer finance.
9. No commas.
10. ..., Crutchfield Industries, ...

Practice Paragraph 4 (page 23)

1. ..., Mr. Black, ...
2. ... Data Products, Inc., ...
3. ... Stephen Gold, Ph.D., ...
4. ..., *Data Jottings*.

Practice Sentences 5 (page 25)

1. ... February 28, 1995.
2. No commas.
3. ... 9 p.m., EST?
4. No commas.
5. ... Thursday, June 12, 1996.
6. No commas.
7. ... November 4, 1994, ...
8. No commas.
9. ... 8:40 a.m., PST.
10. On Wednesday, December 6, 1997, ...

Practice Paragraph 5 (page 25)

1. ... Tuesday, May 3, and Thursday, May 19.
2. ... August 22, 1994.
3. No commas.

Practice Sentences 6 (page 27)

1. ... College, 6201 Winnetka Avenue, Woodland Hills, California 91371.
2. ... Street, Los Angeles, California 90001.
3. ... London, England, and Paris, France, ...
4. ... Honolulu, Hawaii.

5. ... Albuquerque, New Mexico, ...
6. ... Lane, Knoxville, Tennessee 37912.
7. ... Stocker, Office Manager, Smythe & Ryan Investment Counselors, 632 Raven Boulevard, Suite 104, Baltimore, Maryland 21239
8. ... Box 1530, Rural Route 2, Bangor, Maine 55810.
9. Dallas, Texas, ...
10. ... Madrid, Spain.

Practice Paragraph 6 (page 27)

1. ... Hope, Manager, Larry's Clothing Store, 1853 Fountain Avenue, Atlanta, Georgia 30314.
2. ... Columbus, Ohio.
3. ... 9653 Third Avenue, Columbus, Ohio 43203.

Practice Sentences 7 (page 29)

1. ... January, and ....
2. ... 3 p.m., but ....
3. ... office, or ....
4. ... well, nor ....
5. No comma. (Second clause incomplete.)
6. ... published, and ....
7. No comma. (The words *and that* result in a dependent clause.)
8. ... himself, or ....
9. ... Akron, nor ....
10. No comma. (Second clause incomplete.)

Practice Paragraph 7 (page 29)

1. No comma. (Second clause incomplete.)
2. ... office, but ....
3. ... corrected, and ....
4. No comma. (The words *and that* result in a dependent clause.)

Practice Sentences 8 (page 31)

1. ... pleasant, patient ....
2. No commas.
3. No commas.
4. ... elegant, secluded ....
5. No commas.
6. ... ambitious, greedy ....
7. No commas.
8. Your outgoing, cheerful ....
9. ... wealthy, well-known ....
10. No commas.

Practice Paragraph 8 (page 31)

1. Your informative, well-written ....
2. No commas. (... inexpensive modern ....)
3. ... realistic, practical ....

Practice Sentences 9 (page 33)

1. When you see John, ...
2. While you were in New York, ...
3. Before you leave for Denver, ...?
4. As stated previously, ...
5. Because Mr. Logan wishes to move to Indianapolis, ...
6. If so, ...?
7. While Ms. Smith was conferring with her attorney, ...
8. Provided we have an adequate budget, ...
9. If you cannot make an appointment at this time, ...
10. As explained above, ...

Practice Paragraph 9 (page 33)

1. When you receive the material, ...
2. If possible, ...
3. As soon as we receive your corrections, ...
4. ... if the current production schedule is maintained, ...

Practice Sentences 10 (page 35)

1. To continue with this project, ...
2. Seeing that John had made a mistake, ...
3. After viewing the offices in the Hudson Building, ...
4. Near the top of the new listings, ...
5. Tired of her usual routine, ...
6. No comma.
7. No comma.
8. To be interviewed for this position, ...
9. Until the end of the month, ...
10. Encouraged by recent sales increases, ...

Practice Paragraph 10 (page 35)

1. For the past one hundred years, ...
2. No comma.
3. To attract new customers to the Bank of Connecticut, ...
4. Hoping that such an incentive will draw a large group of new depositors, ...

Practice Sentences 11 (page 37)

1. Mr. Sims, who has responsibility for reviewing all appeals, ...
2. No commas.
3. ... article, which appeared in last Sunday's local paper, ...
4. No commas.
5. ... shipped, even though I tried to cancel it.
6. No commas.
7. Mr. Davis, who has attended many of our seminars, ...
8. ... report, which was distributed at the last meeting of department heads.
9. ... Inn, regardless of its expensive meals and remote location.
10. ... president, planning to make major organizational changes, ...

Practice Paragraph 11 (page 37)

1. . . . library, which is located on South Main street, ...
2. No commas.
3. No commas.
4. . . . May 10, before the library opens on May 13.

Practice Sentences 12 (page 39)

1. The format, not the content, ...
2. . . . forms, the sooner we can . . . .
3. . . . July 1, but only to . . . .
4. . . . silver, the greater . . . .
5. . . . report, not just a short memo, outlining . . . .
6. . . . Mary, June 15; Ted, June 22; and Rosa, June 30.
7. . . . yesterday, three; and the day before, two.
8. . . . Department, 12; and the other departments, 8.
9. . . . month, only one.
10. . . . three, in 1998; two, in 1999.

Practice Paragraph 12 (page 39)

1. . . . homes; this week, just four.
2. No commas.
3. . . . plausible, yet weak.
4. No commas.
5. . . . encounters, the more his sales efforts decline.

Practice Sentences 13 (page 41)

1. . . . many, many years.
2. When you work, work . . . .
3. Ever since, Mr. Salazar . . . .
4. We were very, very . . . .
5. The student who cheats, cheats . . . .
6. A long time before, she had spoken . . . .
7. Three months before, our sales manager . . . .
8. Whoever begins, begins . . . .
9. Even before, he had . . . .
10. After this, time will . . . .

Practice Paragraph 13 (page 41)

1. All the meeting was, was a discussion . . . .
2. . . . many, many times.
3. A few weeks before, another committee . . . .
4. Ever since, he has looked . . . .

Practice Sentences 14 (page 43)

1. . . . sign," said Mr. Grey.
2. "How long," asked Ms. Foster, "will it . . . machine?"
3. No commas.
4. Mr. Hughes said, "Everyone . . . ."
5. No commas.
6. "Are you finished," asked Scott, "with . . . ?"

7. The witness reaffirmed, "That . . . ."
8. "Please . . . Friday, May 5," said . . . .
9. No commas.
10. "Mr. David Brown," said Ms. Burns, the Department of Human Resources head, "has . . . ."

Practice Paragraph 14 (page 43)

1. No commas.
2. No commas.
3. . . . asked, "Do you . . . ?"
4. . . . confidently, "I believe . . . ."
5. "I am sure," added Ms. Hill, "that . . . ."

Practice Sentences 15 (page 45)

1. . . . products; we feel . . . .
2. . . . reports; she wishes . . . .
3. Andrea collated, Kim stapled.
4. . . . table; I will . . . .
5. . . . project; he will . . . .
6. I dusted furniture, John cleaned the showcase, Mary vacuumed—all just . . . .
7. . . . meeting; he will . . . .
8. . . . today; the committee . . . .
9. The thief entered, he grabbed the jewels, he exited swiftly.
10. . . . low; they increased somewhat during September; November . . . .

Practice Paragraph 15 (page 45)

1. No commas or semicolons.
2. . . . Green; ask him . . . .
3. He knows Piedmont, he knows commercial real estate, he knows prices.
4. . . . job; Ms. Jones . . . choice; my final . . . .

Practice Sentences 16 (page 47)

1. James Hogan, who is originally from Nevada, has written a book about Las Vegas; and . . . .
2. Cliff Lightfoot, our supervisor, has been ill for several weeks; but he plans to return to the office next Wednesday, November 19.
3. . . . office, and we . . . .
4. We cannot, Ms. Baron, repair the radio under the terms of the warranty; nor . . . . (*or* . . . of the warranty, nor . . . .)
5. Nevertheless, the committee must meet again next Friday; but . . . . (*or* . . . next Friday, but . . . .)
6. . . . nearby, and . . . .
7. . . . engine problems; but according to the latest information we have received, they . . . .
8. I believe, Ms. Edwards, that . . . .
9. You may, of course, wish to keep your original appointment; or . . . . (*or* . . . original appointment, or . . . .)
10. . . . return; but we cannot guarantee that our next program, or any other programs planned for the future, will do so well.

Practice Paragraph 16 (page 47)

1. We were pleased to learn, Mr. Bell, that you have opened a new store on West Main Street; and ....
2. Our new line of stationery, greeting cards, and other paper products should be of interest to you; and we will have our salesman in your area, Jack Dale, phone ....
3. ... you; or he can take you personally to our showroom, which .... (*or* ... you, or he ....)

Practice Sentences 17 (page 49)

1. ... year; therefore, ...
2. ... schedule; however, ...
3. ... remodeling; on the contrary, ...
4. ... wing; consequently, ...
5. ... texts; moreover, ...
6. ... textbook; then we ....
7. ... sharpeners; however, ...
8. Mr. Cooper, vice president of Western Bank, will not be able to attend our meeting; consequently, ...
9. ... hours; thus all ....
10. ... area; therefore, ...

Practice Paragraph 17 (page 49)

1. ... yesterday; however, ...
2. ... May sale; thus we ....
3. No commas or semicolons.

Practice Sentences 18 (page 51)

1. ... Miami, Florida; Houston, Texas; and Portland, Oregon.
2. ... David Stevens, president, North Hills Academy; Agnes Moore, assistant principal, Rhodes School; and Vera Caruso, director, Flintridge Preparatory School.
3. ... campaign; for example, ...
4. ... problem; namely, labor shortages, wage increases, and ....
5. Esther has done all the fact-finding for this case; Jim has verified her findings; and ....
6. ... San Fernando, California; Phoenix, Arizona; and Reno, Nevada, plan to ....
7. ... July 4, 1776; October 24, 1929; and November 22, 1963.
8. ... procedures; for example, we ....
9. ... year; namely, Charles Brubaker, Dana Walters, Phillip Gordon, and Lisa Stanzell.
10. ... Dayton, Ohio; sales territories will be expanded from eight to ten; and ....

Practice Paragraph 18 (page 51)

1. ... London, England; Madrid, Spain; and Frankfurt, Germany.
2. ... European tour; last year we received nearly 400; and ....
3. ... costs; namely, hotel accommodations, meals, and surface transportation.

Practice Sentences 19 (page 53)

1. ... supplies: bond paper, pencils, pens, and writing pads.
2. ... out: Marguerite Rodriguez from Atlas Corporation, Robert Wong from the Accounting Department, Lynne Hale from Thompson Industries, and ....
3. ... viewpoint: she has ....
4. ... bills for January 4, January 8, February 1, and February 7.
5. ... catalogs: Spring 1996 or Summer 1996.

6. ... February were Naomi Chahinian, Bertha Granados, and Kelly Crockett.
7. ... line: shirts, shoes, belts, skirts, and hats.
8. ... year: Belmont ....
9. ... discontinued: we have ....
10. ... sale; namely, 3 cashiers, 5 salespersons, and 6 inventory clerks.

Practice Paragraph 19 (page 53)

1. ... year: Albany, Billings, Dayton, and Fresno.
2. ... San Antonio: the high ....
3. ... home office: Bill Collins, Brad Morgan, Susan Smith, Carol White, and David Williams.

Section 2   Hyphenating and Dividing Words

Practice Guide 1 (page 55)

1. five-minute
2. OK
3. word processing
4. OK
5. alarmingly toxic
6. OK
7. three- and four-bedroom
8. Oklahoma University
9. newly acquired
10. kindhearted
11. thirty-year
12. charge account
13. snow-white
14. OK
15. part-time
16. OK
17. interest-free
18. government sponsored
19. OK
20. air-conditioning
21. high and low selling prices
22. Main Street
23. OK
24. hit-and-miss
25. large- and small-scale
26. redeemable store coupons
27. Little League
28. OK
29. basic accounting
30. home-study

Practice Guide 3 (page 59)

1. nov/elty
2. unde/sir/able
3. ND
4. 4397 Halstead/Street
5. ND
6. ND
7. Mary N./Gomez
8. ND
9. ND
10. Columbus,/Ohio 43210
11. read/ers
12. criti/cal
13. tech/niques
14. ND
15. ND
16. Ms. Darlene/Jackson
17. 3942 East 21/Street
18. December 17,/1996
19. pos/si/ble
20. con/nec/tion
21. brother-/in-/law
22. thor/oughly
23. ND
24. self-/reliance
25. ND

Section 3   Capitalization

Practice Sentences 1 (page 65)

1. Dr. Chu's, Medical Arts Building
2. Promenade Shopping Mall, Franciscan china
3. Caribbean, Viking Queen
4. Green Tree Bridge, Suwannee River
5. Sharp calculators, Dorsey Memocalcs
6. Caesar salad, beef Stroganoff
7. Montclair Hotel, City of Angels
8. venetian blinds
9. Dakota County Fair, Norfolk
10. John Sreveski, india ink

Practice Paragraph 1 (page 65)

1. April, Islands, Alaska, California, Hawaii, Oregon, Washington
2. April, United Airlines, Honolulu
3. American Motors, Ford Motor Company, Budget Car Rental

Practice Sentences 2 (page 67)

1. c.o.d., 2 p.m.
2. CPA, USC
3. Delta Flight 82
4. Invoice 578391
5. page 28, Model 1738 cassette recorder
6. No. 347
7. Figure 3, page 23
8. paragraph 4
9. Policy No. 6429518-C
10. Model No. 17 desk

Practice Paragraph 2 (page 67)

1. policy, No. 846821
2. Section B, paragraph 3
3. Form 6B
4. 9 a.m., 4 p.m.

Practice Sentences 3 (page 69)

1. governor
2. Professor Carlos Rodriguez
3. Mark Swenson, president of Georgetown Steel
4. vice president, Joshua Wooldridge
5. Professor
6. Mayor-elect Ann Brown
7. Byron Teague, assistant dean of instruction
8. personnel director
9. Lieutenant Colonel Bruno Furtado
10. Bill Clinton, the president

Practice Paragraph 3 (page 69)

1. purchasing agents' convention, Miami
2. Mayor Frank Barnes, John Lang, the president of Williams Manufacturing Company
3. Professor Roberta Holt

Practice Sentences 4 (page 71)

1. *A History of the Americas* or <u>A History of the Americas</u> . . . History 12
2. *Music World of Wonder* or<u> Music World of Wonder</u>
3. Theresa Flores, Ph.D., . . . conversational Spanish
4. Walt Disney's movie *The Lion King* or <u>The Lion King</u>
5. Lisa Gartlan, M.D.
6. "A Look at Teenage Life in These United States" . . . *Outlook Magazine* or <u>Outlook Magazine</u>
7. master of science degree in engineering
8. "Singing in the Rain"
9. *The New York Times* or <u>The New York Times</u> . . . *The Wall Street Journal* or <u>The Wall Street Journal</u>
10. Theater Arts 23 . . . *Fiddler on the Roof* or <u>Fiddler on the Roof</u>

Practice Paragraph 4 (page 71)

1. Fred Case, Ph.D., . . . *It's Easy to Make a Million Dollars* or <u>It's Easy to Make a Million Dollars</u>
2. "People Today" . . . *Chronicle* or <u>Chronicle</u>
3. No capitalization
4. *How to Make a Million Without Really Trying* or <u>How to Make a Million Without Really Trying</u> . . . Dr. Case's

Practice Sentences 5 (page 73)

1. National Fund for the Protection of American Wildlife
2. Senate
3. company
4. Accounting Department, Payroll Department
5. Advertising Department
6. county
7. Department of Human Resources
8. government
9. Board of Directors
10. National Council of Teachers of English

Practice Paragraph 5 (page 73)

1. Hughes, Public Relations Department
2. Chamber of Commerce, Rotary Club
3. Fairchild Enterprises

Section 4   Numbers

Practice Sentences 1 (page 77)

1. 27
2. six
3. Thirty-six
4. ten
5. five

6. 38
7. Eighty-six
8. 3 million
9. 25
10. 12

Practice Paragraph 1 (page 77)

1. 75
2. three, twenty or 20

Practice Sentences 2 (page 79)

1. 3
2. 1,000,000
3. 10
4. 11, four
5. 7

6. 382, 9
7. two
8. 8
9. 1 million, 1.5 million
10. four

Practice Paragraph 2 (page 79)

1. 8, 22, 6
2. 9
3. three, two, 13
4. 8, 9, 6

Practice Sentences 3 (page 81)

1. page 7
2. Policy 83478
3. No. 3
4. Number 1886
5. paragraph 8
6. $4
7. 6 percent
8. $.20

9. 8 percent
10. 85 cents
11. 30 cents
12. $1,000,000
13. $4 million
14. 22 percent
15. 0.4

Practice Paragraph 3 (page 81)

1. Policy 7832146
2. page 1, line 6, $47,000
3. $168
4. 8 percent

Practice Sentences 4 (page 83)

1. 9 pounds 12 ounces
2. 3
3. June 3
4. 6 p.m.
5. 8 inches
6. 4 pounds 2 ounces
7. October 25
8. 9 o'clock in the morning
9. 1st of January
10. eighteen
11. 30
12. 18
13. thirty-three
14. 125th
15. 63

Practice Paragraph 4 (page 83)

1. August 13, August 24, 116 degrees
2. 25th of August, 110 degrees
3. twelve-day

Section 5   Abbreviations and Contractions

Practice Guide 1 (page 85)

1. CST
2. 900 B.C.
3. CLU
4. OK
5. NBC
6. Dr.
7. OK
8. OK
9. Model No. 1417
10. c.o.d.
11. OK
12. Ext. 327
13. U.K.
14. N.E.
15. Brig. Gen. Ret. Foster L. Klein
16. etc.
17. OK
18. M.D.
19. Ralph T. Drengson Sr.
20. IBM PS2

Practice Guide 3 (page 88)

1. OK
2. I'm not
3. isn't
4. OK
5. You're
6. hasn't
7. OK
8. its
9. they're
10. OK

Section 6 Literary and Artistic Titles

Practice Guide 1 (page 89)

1. b and e
2. e
3. d
4. b
5. e

6. a
7. b
8. b and d
9. c
10. d

Section 7 Words Often Misused and Confused

Practice Exercises for Selected Words From *A/An* Through *Aisle/Isle*

Practice Guide 1 (pages 93–96)

A/An

1. an
2. a
3. a
4. an
5. a

A while/Awhile

6. a while
7. awhile
8. A while
9. a while
10. awhile

Accede/Exceed

11. exceed
12. accede
13. exceed
14. accede
15. exceed

Accept/Except

16. accept
17. except
18. except
19. accept
20. accepted

Access/Excess

21. access
22. excess
23. excess
24. access
25. access

Ad/Add

26. add
27. add
28. ad
29. add
30. ad

Adapt/Adept/Adopt

31. adopt
32. adapt
33. adept
34. adapt
35. adopt

Addict/Edict

36. addicts
37. edict
38. edict
39. addicts
40. edict

Addition/Edition

41. edition
42. additions
43. addition
44. editions
45. edition

Adherence/Adherents

46. Adherence
47. adherence
48. adherents
49. adherents
50. adherence

Adverse/Averse

51. averse
52. adverse
53. averse
54. Adverse
55. averse

Advice/Advise

56. advise
57. advice
58. advice
59. advice
60. advise

Affect/Effect

61. effect
62. affect
63. effect
64. affect
65. effect

Aisle/Isle

71. aisle
72. aisles
73. isle
74. isle
75. aisle

Aid/Aide

66. aid
67. aid
68. aide
69. aid
70. aides

Reinforcement Guide 1 (pages 97–98)

1. advice
2. edict
3. accept
4. aisle
5. averse
6. adapt
7. exceed
8. aid
9. adherence
10. access
11. awhile
12. affect
13. additions
14. ad
15. a
16. adverse
17. adept
18. accede
19. effect
20. exceed

Practice Exercises for Selected Words From *Allowed/Aloud* Through *Any Way/Anyway*

Practice Guide 2 (pages 99–103)

Allowed/Aloud

1. allowed
2. allowed
3. aloud
4. allowed
5. aloud

All ready/Already

6. all ready
7. already
8. already
9. already
10. all ready

All right/Alright

11. all right
12. all right
13. all right
14. all right
15. all right

All together/Altogether

16. altogether
17. all together
18. all together
19. altogether
20. altogether

Allude/Elude

21. allude
22. elude
23. allude
24. elude
25. allude

Allusion/Delusion/Illusion

26. illusion
27. illusion
28. delusion
29. allusion
30. illusion

All Ways/Always

31. always
32. always
33. all ways
34. always
35. all ways

Almost/Most

36. Almost
37. Most
38. almost
39. almost
40. almost

Altar/Alter

41. alter
42. altars
43. altar
44. alter
45. alter

Among/Between

46. among
47. between
48. between
49. between
50. among

Amount/Number

51. number
52. number
53. number
54. amount
55. number

Anecdote/Antidote

56. anecdote
57. anecdote
58. antidote
59. antidotes
60. anecdotes

Annual/Annul

61. annul
62. annual
63. annual
64. annual
65. annual

Any one/Anyone

66. anyone
67. Any one
68. any one
69. Anyone
70. anyone

Any time/Anytime

71. Any time
72. anytime
73. anytime
74. any time
75. any time

Any way/Anyway

76. anyway
77. Any way
78. any way
79. any way
80. Anyway

Reinforcement Guide 2 (pages 103–104)

1. any way
2. antidote
3. almost
4. altogether
5. any time
6. number
7. always
8. all right
9. anyone
10. among
11. illusion
12. all ready
13. annul
14. alter
15. allude
16. allowed
17. delusion
18. elude
19. any one
20. between

Practice Exercises for Selected Words From *Appraise/Apprise* Through *Born/Borne*

Practice Guide 3 (pages 105–108)

Appraise/Apprise

1. apprise
2. apprised
3. appraised
4. appraise
5. apprised

As/Like

6. as
7. like
8. as
9. like
10. As

Ascent/Assent

11. ascent
12. assent
13. ascent
14. ascent
15. assent

Assistance/Assistants

16. assistance
17. assistance
18. assistance
19. assistants
20. assistants

Assure/Ensure/Insure

21. ensure
22. insure
23. ensure
24. assure
25. assure

Attendance/Attendants

26. attendance
27. attendance
28. attendants
29. attendance
30. attendants

Bad/Badly

31. bad
32. badly
33. badly
34. bad
35. bad

Bail/Bale

36. bales
37. bail
38. bail
39. bales
40. bales

Bare/Bear

41. bare
42. bear
43. bare
44. bare
45. bare

Base/Bass

46. bass
47. base
48. base
49. base
50. bass

Beside/Besides

51. besides
52. beside
53. beside
54. besides
55. besides

Biannual/Biennial

56. biannual
57. biannual
58. Biennial
59. biannual
60. biennially

Billed/Build

61. billed
62. build
63. build
64. build
65. billed

Bolder/Boulder

66. bolder
67. boulder
68. bolder
69. bolder
70. boulders

Born/Borne

71. borne
72. borne
73. born
74. borne
75. born

Reinforcement Guide 3 (pages 109–110)

1. borne
2. besides
3. bad
4. As
5. biennial
6. bale
7. bare
8. billed
9. apprise
10. ascent
11. assistance
12. ensure
13. attendance
14. base
15. bolder
16. appraise
17. assents
18. ensure
19. badly
20. biannually

Practice Exercises for Selected Words From *Bouillon/Bullion* Through *Coarse/Course*

Practice Guide 4 (pages 111–114)

Bouillon/Bullion

1. bouillon
2. bullion
3. bullion
4. bouillon
5. bouillon

Breach/Breech

6. breach
7. breached
8. breech
9. breach
10. breach

Callous/Callus

11. callous
12. callous
13. callus
14. callous
15. callus

Can/May

16. may
17. may
18. can
19. Can
20. may

Canvas/Canvass

21. canvas
22. canvass
23. canvas
24. canvass
25. canvass

Capital/Capitol

26. capital
27. capitol
28. capital
29. capital
30. Capitol

Carat/Caret/Carrot/Karat

31. carat
32. karat, karat
33. caret
34. carrot
35. karat

Cease/Seize

36. cease
37. cease
38. seize
39. seize
40. cease

Censor/Censure

41. censor
42. censure
43. censured
44. censors
45. censored

Census/Senses

46. senses
47. census
48. census
49. census
50. senses

Cent/Scent/Sent

51. cent
52. sent
53. scents
54. scent
55. cent

Cereal/Serial

56. serial
57. cereals
58. cereal
59. serial
60. serial

Choose/Chose

61. chose
62. choose
63. choose
64. chose
65. choose

Cite/Sight/Site

66. site
67. cite
68. sight
69. cited
70. sites

Coarse/Course

71. course
72. course
73. coarse
74. course
75. course

Reinforcement Guide 4 (pages 115–116)

1. serial
2. cease
3. may
4. coarse
5. scent
6. caret
7. callous
8. site
9. census
10. capitol
11. breach
12. choose
13. censured
14. canvass
15. bouillon
16. capital
17. cite
18. capital
19. sights
20. censor

Practice Exercises for Selected Words From *Collision/Collusion* Through *Deference/Difference*

Practice Guide 5 (pages 117–121)

Collision/Collusion

1. collusion
2. collision
3. collusion
4. collision
5. collusion

Command/Commend

6. commend
7. commended
8. commands
9. command
10. commend

Complement/Compliment

11. complement
12. complement
13. complement
14. compliments
15. compliment

Complementary/ Complimentary

16. complimentary
17. complementary
18. complementary
19. complimentary
20. complimentary

Confidant/Confident

21. confidant
22. confident
23. confident
24. confidant
25. confident

Conscience/Conscious

26. conscience
27. conscious
28. conscience
29. conscious
30. conscious

Console/Consul

31. console
32. consoles
33. consul
34. console
35. consul

Continual/Continuous

36. continual
37. continually
38. continuous
39. continuously
40. continually

Cooperation/Corporation

41. cooperation
42. corporation
43. cooperation
44. cooperation
45. corporations

Corespondent/Correspondence/ Correspondent

46. corespondent
47. correspondence
48. correspondents
49. correspondence
50. correspondents

Corps/Corpse

51. corpse
52. corps
53. Corps
54. corpse
55. corps

Council/Counsel

56. council
57. counsel
58. council
59. council
60. counsels

Credible/Creditable

61. creditable
62. creditable
63. creditable
64. credible
65. credible

Decent/Descent/Dissent

66. descent
67. decent
68. Dissent
69. descent
70. dissent

Defer/Differ

71. defer
72. differ
73. defer
74. defer
75. differ

Deference/Difference

76. deference
77. difference
78. difference
79. difference
80. deference

Reinforcement Guide 5 (pages 121–122)

1. complimentary
2. continual
3. council
4. deference
5. collusion
6. confidant
7. corporation
8. creditable
9. commend
10. conscious
11. correspondence
12. descent
13. complementary
14. consoles
15. corps
16. defer
17. complement
18. continuously
19. counsel
20. credible

Practice Exercises for Selected Words From *Deprecate/Depreciate* Through *Expansive/Expensive*

Practice Guide 6 (pages 123–127)

Deprecate/Depreciate

1. deprecate
2. depreciate
3. depreciates
4. deprecate
5. depreciate

Desert/Dessert

6. desert
7. desert
8. desserts
9. dessert
10. dessert

Device/Devise

11. devise
12. devise
13. device
14. devise
15. device

Dew/Do/Due

16. due
17. dew
18. do
19. due
20. due

Disapprove/Disprove

21. disapprove
22. disprove
23. disprove
24. disapproves
25. disapprove

Disburse/Disperse

26. disperse
27. disbursed
28. disburse
29. dispersed
30. disburse

Done/Dun

31. dun
32. dun
33. done
34. dun
35. dun

Elicit/Illicit

36. elicit
37. elicit
38. illicit
39. elicit
40. illicit

Emigrate/Immigrate

41. emigrated
42. emigrated
43. immigrate
44. emigrated
45. immigrate

Eminent/Imminent

46. eminent
47. eminent
48. imminent
49. imminent
50. imminent

Envelop/Envelope

51. envelope
52. envelops
53. enveloped
54. envelop
55. envelopes

Every day/Everyday

56. Every day
57. Everyday
58. Every day
59. everyday
60. every day

Every one/Everyone

61. Everyone
62. Every one
63. everyone
64. everyone
65. every one

Executioner/Executor

66. executor
67. executor
68. executioner
69. executioner
70. executor

Expand/Expend

71. expend
72. expand
73. expand
74. expand
75. expand

Expansive/Expensive

76. Expansive
77. expensive
78. expensive
79. expensive
80. expansive

Reinforcement Guide 6 (pages 127–128)

1. everyone
2. emigrated
3. disapproves
4. deprecate
5. executor
6. imminent
7. disperse
8. dessert
9. expend
10. envelop
11. dun
12. devise
13. expansive
14. every day
15. elicit
16. due
17. disbursed
18. immigrate
19. Eminent
20. everyday

Practice Exercises for Selected Words From *Explicit/Implicit* Through *Former/Latter*

Practice Guide 7 (pages 129–133)

Explicit/Implicit

1. implicit
2. explicitly
3. Explicit
4. implicitly
5. explicit

Extant/Extent

6. extent
7. extant
8. extant
9. extent
10. extant

Facetious/Factious

11. facetious
12. facetious
13. factious
14. factious
15. facetious

Factitious/Fictitious

16. fictitious
17. factitious
18. factitious
19. fictitious
20. fictitious

Fair/Fare

21. fare
22. fair
23. fair
24. fair
25. fare

Farther/Further

26. further
27. farther
28. further
29. farther
30. farther

Feat/Fete

31. fete
32. feats
33. feat
34. fete
35. feted

Fewer/Less

36. fewer
37. fewer
38. less
39. fewer
40. Fewer

Finally/Finely

41. finally
42. finely
43. finely
44. finally
45. finally

Flagrant/Fragrant

46. flagrant
47. flagrant
48. fragrant
49. flagrant
50. fragrant

Flair/Flare

51. flair
52. flair
53. flare
54. flare
55. Flared

Flaunt/Flout

56. flaunt
57. flout
58. flouting
59. flout
60. flaunting

Flew/Flu/Flue

61. flue
62. flu
63. flue
64. flew
65. flu

Formally/Formerly

66. formally
67. formerly
68. formerly
69. formally
70. formally

Former/Latter

71. former
72. former
73. latter
74. former
75. latter

Reinforcement Guide 7 (pages 133–134)

1. former
2. extant
3. further
4. fete
5. flared
6. flouts
7. factitious
8. implicit
9. fares
10. flair
11. fewer
12. formerly
13. Flagrant
14. finely
15. factious
16. flue
17. explicit
18. fictitious
19. facetious
20. flaunted

Practice Exercises for Selected Words From *Forth/Fourth* Through *Imply/Infer*

Practice Guide 8 (pages 135–139)

Forth/Fourth

1. fourth
2. forth
3. fourth
4. fourth
5. forth

Good/Well

6. well
7. well
8. good
9. good
10. well

Grate/Great

11. great
12. grate
13. grate
14. grate
15. great

Guarantee/Guaranty

16. guaranty
17. guarantee
18. guarantee
19. guaranty
20. guarantee

He/Him/Himself

21. him
22. he
23. himself
24. he
25. him

Hear/Here

26. here
27. here
28. hear
29. hear
30. here

Her/Herself/She

31. herself
32. she
33. her
34. she
35. she

Hew/Hue

36. hewed
37. hues
38. hue
39. hew
40. hue

Hoard/Horde

41. Hordes
42. horde
43. hoard
44. hoard
45. hoard

Hole/Whole

46. hole
47. whole
48. whole
49. holes
50. whole

Holy/Wholly

51. wholly
52. holy
53. wholly
54. wholly
55. wholly

Human/Humane

56. human
57. human
58. Humane
59. human
60. humane

Hypercritical/Hypocritical

61. Hypercritical
62. hypercritical
63. hypocritical
64. hypercritical
65. hypocritical

I/Me/Myself

66. me
67. I
68. I
69. me
70. I

Ideal/Idle/Idol

71. idle
72. idol
73. ideal
74. idle
75. ideal

Imply/Infer

76. imply
77. imply
78. inferred
79. infer
80. implied

Reinforcement Guide 8 (pages 139–140)

1. hypercritical
2. hoard
3. he
4. forth
5. me
6. whole
7. hear
8. well
9. idle
10. wholly
11. her
12. grates
13. infer
14. human
15. hewed
16. guaranty
17. imply
18. hypocritical
19. well
20. horde

Practice Exercises for Selected Words From *Incidence/Incidents* Through *Liable/Libel*

Practice Guide 9 (pages 141–144)

Incidence/Incidents

1. incidents
2. incidences
3. incidence
4. incidents
5. incidences

Incite/Insight

6. incite
7. incited
8. insight
9. insight
10. incite

Indigenous/Indigent/Indignant

11. indigenous
12. indigent
13. Indigents
14. indignant
15. indigenous

Ingenious/Ingenuous

16. Ingenious
17. ingenious
18. ingenuous
19. ingenious
20. ingenuous

Interstate/Intrastate

21. intrastate
22. interstate
23. interstate
24. interstate
25. intrastate

Its/It's

26. it's
27. its
28. it's
29. its
30. its

Later/Latter

31. latter
32. later
33. later
34. latter
35. latter

Lay/Lie

36. lie
37. lain
38. lay
39. lying
40. lies

Lean/Lien

41. lean
42. leans
43. liens
44. lean
45. lien

Leased/Least

46. least
47. least
48. leased
49. leased
50. leased

Lend/Loan

51. loan
52. lend
53. lend
54. loan
55. lend

Lessee/Lesser/Lessor

56. lessor
57. lessee
58. lessor
59. lesser
60. lesser

Lessen/Lesson

61. lessen
62. lessened
63. lesson
64. lessen
65. lesson

Levee/Levy

66. levees
67. levy
68. levy
69. levee
70. levies

Liable/Libel

71. liable
72. liable
73. libel
74. libelous
75. liable

Reinforcement Guide 9 (pages 145–146)

1. lessee
2. lie
3. ingenuous
4. lend
5. liable
6. latter
7. indigenous
8. levy
9. leased
10. its
11. incite
12. lessen
13. lien
14. intrastate
15. incidence(s)
16. libel
17. indigent
18. lie
19. ingenious
20. interstate

Practice Exercises for Selected Words From *Lightening/Lightning* Through *Overdo/Overdue*

Practice Guide 10 (pages 147–150)

Lightening/Lightning

1. lightening
2. lightening
3. lightning
4. lightening
5. lightning

Local/Locale

6. Local
7. locale
8. locale
9. local
10. local

Loose/Lose

11. lose
12. loose
13. lose
14. loose
15. lose

Magnate/Magnet

16. magnet
17. magnate
18. magnate
19. magnet
20. magnetic

Main/Mane

21. main
22. main
23. mane
24. main
25. mane

Manner/Manor

26. manner
27. manors
28. manor
29. manner
30. manner

Marital/Marshal/Martial

31. marital
32. marshal
33. martial
34. marshal
35. marital

May be/Maybe

36. may be
37. Maybe
38. maybe
39. may be
40. may be

Medal/Meddle

41. meddle
42. medal
43. medal
44. meddle
45. meddle

Miner/Minor

46. minor
47. minor
48. miner
49. minors
50. minor

Mode/Mood

51. mood
52. mode
53. mode
54. mode
55. mood

Moral/Morale

56. morale
57. morale
58. moral
59. moral
60. morale

Morning/Mourning

61. morning
62. morning
63. mourning
64. morning
65. mourning

Naval/Navel

66. naval
67. navel
68. navel
69. naval
70. naval

Ordinance/Ordnance

71. ordinance
72. ordinances
73. ordnance
74. ordnance
75. ordinances

Overdo/Overdue

76. overdue
77. overdo
78. overdo
79. overdue
80. overdue

Reinforcement Guide 10 (pages 151–152)

1. morale
2. martial
3. locale
4. mourning
5. may be
6. lose
7. naval
8. medal
9. magnate
10. ordinance
11. minor
12. mane
13. overdue
14. mode
15. manor
16. Lightning
17. meddle
18. marshal
19. magnet
20. lightening

Practice Exercises for Selected Words From *Pair/Pare/Pear* Through *Practicable/Practical*

Practice Guide 11 (pages 153–156)

Pair/Pare/Pear

1. pare
2. pear
3. pairs
4. pare
5. pair

Partition/Petition

6. petition
7. partition
8. partitioned
9. partition
10. petition

Passed/Past

11. past
12. passed
13. past
14. passed
15. past

Patience/Patients

16. patients
17. patience
18. patients
19. patients
20. patience

Peace/Piece

21. peace
22. peace
23. piece
24. peace
25. pieces

Peal/Peel

26. peal
27. peals
28. peel
29. pealed
30. peeling

Peer/Pier

31. peer
32. peers
33. pier
34. peer
35. pier

Persecute/Prosecute

36. persecute
37. persecuted
38. prosecute
39. persecute
40. prosecuted

Personal/Personnel

41. personnel
42. personnel
43. personal
44. personnel
45. personal

Perspective/Prospective

46. perspective
47. prospective
48. prospective
49. perspective
50. perspective

Plaintiff/Plaintive

51. plaintiff
52. plaintiffs
53. plaintive
54. plaintiff
55. plaintive

Pole/Poll

56. pole
57. poll
58. poles
59. poll
60. polls

Populace/Populous

61. populace
62. populous
63. populous
64. populace
65. populace

Pore/Pour

66. pores
67. pore
68. pour
69. poured
70. poring

Practicable/Practical

71. practicable
72. practical
73. practical
74. practicable
75. practical

Reinforcement Guide 11 (pages 157–158)

1. poll
2. persecute
3. patience
4. practicable
5. plaintive
6. peer
7. past
8. pore
9. perspective
10. peal
11. petition
12. populous
13. personnel
14. piece
15. pare
16. plaintiff
17. pour
18. partition
19. prospective
20. populace

Practice Exercises for Selected Words From *Pray/Prey* Through *Scene/Seen*

Practice Guide 12 (pages 159–163)

Pray/Prey

1. prey
2. pray
3. pray
4. prey
5. prey

Precede/Proceed

6. proceed
7. precede
8. precede
9. preceded
10. proceed

Precedence/Precedents

11. precedence
12. precedence
13. precedents
14. precedent
15. precedence

Presence/Presents

16. presents
17. presence
18. presence
19. presents
20. presence

Principal/Principle

21. principal
22. principal
23. principal
24. principle
25. principle

Propose/Purpose

26. propose
27. purpose
28. purpose
29. proposed
30. propose

Quiet/Quite

31. quiet
32. quite
33. quite
34. quiet
35. quite

Raise/Raze/Rise

36. rise
37. raze
38. raise
39. rose
40. razed

Real/Really

41. really
42. really
43. real
44. real
45. really

Reality/Realty

46. realty
47. reality
48. realty
49. reality
50. realty

Receipt/Recipe

51. receipt
52. recipe
53. recipes
54. receipt
55. receipt

Residence/Residents

56. Residents
57. residence
58. residence
59. residents
60. residents

Respectably/Respectfully/ Respectively

61. respectfully
62. respectively
63. respectfully
64. respectably
65. respectively

Role/Roll

66. Roll
67. role
68. roll
69. role
70. roll

Rote/Rout/Route

71. rote
72. routed
73. route
74. rote
75. route

Scene/Seen

76. seen
77. scene
78. scene
79. seen
80. seen

Reinforcement Guide 12 (pages 163–164)

1. respectively
2. really or quite
3. principle
4. prey
5. role
6. realty
7. propose
8. proceed
9. rote
10. receipt
11. quite
12. precedence
13. scene
14. residents
15. raze
16. presence
17. principal
18. precedent
19. rout
20. rise

Practice Exercises for Selected Words From *Set/Sit* Through *Sure/Surely*

Practice Guide 13 (pages 165–168)

Set/Sit

1. set
2. sit
3. sat
4. setting
5. sitting

Sew/So/Sow

6. sow
7. so
8. sown
9. sew
10. sewing

Shall/Will

11. will
12. will
13. will
14. will
15. will

Shear/Sheer

16. sheer
17. sheer
18. sheared
19. sheer
20. shear

Shone/Shown

21. shone
22. shown
23. shown
24. shone
25. shone

Should/Would

26. would
27. should
28. should
29. would
30. should

Soar/Sore

31. soar
32. sore
33. soared
34. soaring
35. sore

Sole/Soul

36. sole
37. sole
38. soul
39. soul
40. sole

Some/Somewhat

41. somewhat
42. some
43. some
44. somewhat
45. some

Some time/Sometime

46. sometime
47. sometime
48. some time
49. sometime
50. some time

Staid/Stayed

51. stayed
52. staid
53. stayed
54. staid
55. stayed

Stationary/Stationery

56. stationery
57. stationery
58. stationary
59. stationery
60. stationary

Statue/Stature/Statute

61. stature
62. statue
63. Statutes
64. statue
65. stature

Straight/Strait

66. straight
67. strait
68. straight
69. Strait
70. straight

Suit/Suite

71. suite
72. suit
73. suite
74. suite
75. suit

Sure/Surely

76. surely
77. sure
78. surely
79. surely
80. sure

Reinforcement Guide 13 (pages 169–170)

1. statute
2. somewhat
3. shone
4. set
5. strait
6. sometime
7. would
8. sews
9. suite
10. staid
11. soar
12. will
13. surely
14. stationery
15. soul
16. sheer
17. stationary
18. stature
19. sole
20. suit

Practice Exercises for Selected Words From *Tare/Tear/Tier* Through *Your/You're*

Practice Guide 14 (pages 171–174)

Tare/Tear/Tier

1. tare
2. tier
3. tear
4. tare
5. tier

Than/Then

6. than
7. than
8. then
9. then
10. than

That/Which

11. that
12. which
13. which
14. that
15. that

Their/There/They're

16. they're
17. there
18. they're
19. their
20. their

Them/They

21. they
22. they
23. they
24. them
25. they

Threw/Through

26. threw
27. through
28. through
29. threw
30. through

To/Too/Two

31. too
32. too
33. too
34. to
35. Too

Us/We

36. us
37. we
38. we
39. us
40. we

Vain/Van/Vane/Vein

41. vain
42. vane
43. vans
44. vain
45. vein

Vary/Very

46. very
47. vary
48. vary
49. very
50. vary

Waive/Wave

51. wave
52. waive
53. waving
54. waived
55. wave

Waiver/Waver

56. waiver
57. waver
58. wavered
59. waiver
60. wavered

Weather/Whether

61. weather
62. whether
63. whether
64. weather
65. weather

Who/Whom

66. who
67. whom
68. Whom
69. Who
70. whom

Who's/Whose

71. who's
72. whose
73. whose
74. who's
75. who's

Your/You're

76. you're
77. your
78. your
79. you're
80. You're

Reinforcement Guide 14 (pages 175–176)

1. whether
2. vain
3. they
4. tare
5. whom
6. vary
7. through
8. than
9. who's
10. waive
11. too
12. which
13. you're
14. waver
15. us
16. their
17. whose
18. waiver
19. tiers
20. veins

Additional Practice Exercises for *Affect/Effect*

Practice Guide 15, Part A (page 177)

1. effect
2. affect
3. affect
4. effecting
5. effect
6. affect
7. effect
8. effect
9. effect
10. effects
11. affect
12. affect
13. effect
14. effecting
15. effect

Practice Guide 15, Part B (page 178)

1. effect
2. affect
3. effect
4. effect
5. affected
6. effect
7. effected
8. affected
9. effect
10. effect
11. effect
12. affected
13. effects
14. affected
15. effect
16. effect
17. affect
18. effect
19. effect
20. affect

Reinforcement Guide 15 (page 179)

We have not yet been able to determine what *effect* our new pricing policy will have on sales. With the present sales volume, we can only predict that unless our manager, Mr. Jones, can *effect* significant cost reductions, this pricing policy will result in declining profits. If, on the other hand, the *effect* of our present sales campaign escalates our sales volume, then we can expect the new pricing policy to be successful. In summary, sales volume and costs will *affect* directly the new pricing structure initiated by Mr. Jones.

During the next quarter we will be able to analyze the overall *effect* of the new policy and how it has *affected* our profit picture. Before Mr. Jones is permitted to *effect* any additional changes, though, the Board of Directors must review carefully how any new recommendations will *affect* our entire operation in light of the potential problems that may exist with our new pricing policy. Too many unprecedented policy decisions could *affect* adversely the price of our stock, and we might encounter difficulty in *effecting* changes to restore the price to its normal high level.

Cumulative Practice Guides

Cumulative Practice Guide 1 (pages 181–182)

1. an
2. accept
3. adapt
4. advice
5. affect
6. already
7. altogether
8. elude
9. Almost
10. among
11. anyone
12. as
13. ensure
14. badly
15. biannually
16. capitol
17. site
18. complements
19. continual
20. council
21. dissent
22. deprecate
23. devise
24. due
25. disperse

Cumulative Practice Guide 2 (pages 182–183)

1. elicit
2. emigrated
3. imminent
4. every day
5. everyone
6. further
7. fewer
8. formerly
9. well
10. hoard
11. me
12. imply
13. indigent
14. interstate
15. its
16. lie
17. liable
18. loose
19. martial
20. Maybe
21. morale
22. overdue
23. passed
24. patience
25. persecuting

Cumulative Practice Guide 3 (pages 183–184)

1. personal
2. prospective
3. proceed
4. precedence
5. principle
6. quiet
7. rise
8. really
9. realty
10. receipt
11. respectfully
12. route
13. set
14. sew
15. sheer
16. sometime
17. stationary
18. stature
19. surely
20. than
21. their
22. too
23. waver
24. whether
25. You're

Section 8   Grammar and Usage

Noun Plurals

Practice Guide 1 (page 197)

1. policies
2. churches
3. radios
4. lives
5. Montgomerys
6. tomatoes
7. curricula
8. statistics
9. mumps
10. brigadier generals
11. yeses and noes
12. cupfuls
13. bookshelves
14. brothers-in-law
15. bases
16. pants
17. 9s
18. roofs
19. attorneys
20. waltzes
21. altos
22. cargoes
23. thises and thats
24. monkeys
25. analyses
26. alumni
27. per diems
28. counties
29. boxes
30. Koltzes
31. A's
32. bronchi
33. lessees
34. father figures
35. fathers-in-law
36. valleys
37. R.N.s
38. Mses. Ross *or* Ms. Rosses
39. data
40. Mickey Mouses
41. goings-over
42. t's
43. jockeys
44. Japanese
45. Messrs. Ramirez *or* Mr. Ramirezes
46. embargoes
47. yourselves
48. chassis
49. halves
50. Germans

Noun Possessives

Practice Guide 3 (page 199)

1. son-in-law's
2. children's
3. Everyone else's
4. week's
5. personnel managers'
6. Rosses and Lopezes'
7. girls'
8. Mr. Beaty's
9. Bob's and Phil's
10. company's
11. ladies'
12. months'
13. Mary's
14. Jones's
15. chief of police's
16. Alumni's
17. ITT's
18. expiration date of the lease
19. men's and boys'
20. Martha and Don's

Pronouns

Practice Guide 5 (pages 201–202)

Part 1

1. We
2. me
3. he
4. I
5. she
6. us
7. he
8. me
9. her
10. I

Part 2

1. Between you and me, ...
2. . . . was *she*?
3. . . . to be *she* . . . .
4. . . . have been *he.*
5. . . . Paul and *me.*
6. . . . Teri and *me* . . . .
7. OK
8. . . . Bob, Arlene, and *I* . . . .
9. If you were *I,* . . . ?
10. OK

Part 3

1. who
2. whom
3. who
4. who
5. Whoever
6. who
7. Whom
8. whoever
9. who
10. whom
11. Whoever
12. who
13. whom
14. whom
15. who

Verbs

Practice Guide 7 (page 205)

1. Have you <u>written</u> letters to the two agencies?
2. The tract of new homes <u>was</u> laid out attractively.
3. Our client has already <u>spoken</u> to several agents in your firm.
4. The patient asked if he could <u>lie</u> down on the cot.
5. <u>Have</u> the criteria been ranked in the order of their importance?
6. There <u>are</u> several alternatives you may wish to consider.
7. Neither of us <u>wishes</u> to postpone his vacation.
8. OK
9. Dr. Sanders is one of those doctors who <u>know</u> a great deal about law.
10. Our stock of felt-tip pens <u>has</u> disappeared from the supply cabinet.
11. He had <u>forgotten</u> about this appointment until his secretary reminded him.
12. Until last Wednesday the books had <u>lain</u> on top of the counter.
13. All the juice in these bottles <u>has</u> been drunk.
14. OK
15. Neither you nor the other accountant <u>has</u> been absent this year.
16. OK
17. The staff <u>were</u> arguing loudly about their duties. (*or* The staff members <u>were</u> . . . .)
18. One of the mothers <u>has</u> consented to bring donuts for the class.
19. All our bills for this month have been <u>paid.</u>
20. OK